The Bible Understood

Unlock God's story and find your place in it

Kim West PhD MDiv

Bold Faith Press

ISBN: 979-8-9904571-0-2 (sc)

ISBN: 979-8-9904571-1-9 (e)

Library of Congress Control Number: 2024936985

Printed in the United States of America

FIRST EDITION

By Kim West, PhD, M.Div. – 1st Ed.

Bold Faith Press
Payson, AZ

THE BIBLE UNDERSTOOD

CONTENTS

PREFACE

In January of 2000 I had the privilege or going to Nairobi with a team from Phoenix Seminary. I had been asked to be one of the teachers at a conference for Christian women leaders from Kenya, Tanzania and Uganda.

Over the course of five days one of the subjects I taught was the overview of the entire Bible. With a flip chart and my Bible, I taught from Genesis to Revelation the big story of God's love and redemption. It was a powerful time and I loved every minute of it.

Their hunger to know God and His Word was incredible. To teach these women was humbling and joyous.

I left all of my notes (and my flip chart) with the women who asked for them. Upon my return home, I rewrote the content into this book. I have taught it online and in person several times since then and it is always one of my most favorite courses that I teach.

To understand the Bible is to understand life. It gives meaning and purpose to our days. It brings joy and rest to the soul and it empowers and prepares us for eternity. Understanding God's Word is how we connect with our holy God and know how to live with and before Him.

***

If you would like to use this book as a group study, I have a video course that goes along with this book. You can find it at https://courses.drkimwest.info/courses/the-bible-un derstood

INTRODUCTION

Sixty-six books written by forty authors in three different languages over a period of time of 1600 years on three different continents – this is the Bible. With all of that, there is only one story that runs through all sixty-six books of the Bible.

THE story is the person of God and His love and interaction with mankind as He brings eternal redemption through His Son Jesus Christ so that we might know Him and adore Him forever.

But with all of the books and people and events sometimes that one story gets lost.

There are a lot of characters in this Biblical story. Think of some: Noah, Isaiah, Joshua, Abraham, Paul, Miriam, and Deborah. Could you place them in a Biblical timeline and know how the Lord was working through them in His story and for His eternal purposes?

The Big Picture of the Big Story

If we are to look at the world from above, we will understand how a particular river weaves its way through the land and finally joins with the ocean. We will understand how a mountain range divides a continent and separates peoples and cultures. We will see forests and deserts, farm lands and bodies of waters. With this big picture we will know the terrain, all the parts of the land and how to navigate within the territory. This book is the same method.

This is how we will learn God's story, keep the big picture in mind, and to be able to place people and events within the story. I encourage you to go deeper into the Bible after you have finished this overview by looking deeply into each book of the Bible independently.

This book will help you to praise and worship God for His magnificent plan as you see His loving hand throughout His story.

How to use this book.

Our study is broken into four sections with a total of 16 lessons that will help you to keep the whole Biblical picture in mind as well as be able to place people and events within that big picture.

Each of the 16 lessons starts with the letter "C" which helps you to learn and remember the flow of Scripture.

Each lesson starts with a graphic that tells you the Scriptures to be read, the main characters in the section and the events that happen.

Review the section titles and events as you go and by the end of the book you will not only see the big picture but know how it fits together to God's glory.

Section 1 - Adam to Abraham

In this section we start with Adam, the first man, and end with Abraham, with whom God makes a covenant of salvation and hope. This Abrahamic Covenant then guides our understanding of the rest of the Bible. There are five titles in this section.

- Creation

- Consequences

- Corruption

- Confusion

- Covenant

Practice memorizing these first five titles. Remember the main events and people in each as you repeat them.

Section 2 - From a Family to a Nation

God builds Abraham and his family into a nation through whom will come the Savior for all mankind. There are three titles in this section.

- Captivity 1

- Camp

- Conquest

Practice adding these three titles to the five you memorized already. Once memorized, if I were to ask you where Noah or Joseph or Joshua fall you should be able to tell me where and when.

Section 3 - King Saul to Christ the King

God's people wanted a king to rule over them and they have many but God always had in mind that His Son would rule as King over all creation. There are four titles in this section.

- Crown

- Captivity 2

- Construction

- Christ

Add these four C-titles to those you have memorized.

Section 4 – The Church on Earth to the Heavenly Kingdom

We are at the final stages of the redemption story. The body of Christ awaits His return and the completion of the work God started way back in Creation. There are four titles in this final section.

- Church

- Christ Returns

- Christ the King

- Completion

You should understand the whole story of the Bible now and be able to place people and events within their respective sections.

***

Note: I came across an old book many decades ago that had broken Scripture into sections starting with the letter "C." This book is based upon that format.[1]

---

1. Bible History Visualized, Ray Baughman, 1963

Section 1 – Adam to Abraham

We begin our study with God.

All of the Bible, all of life is about Him, for Him and because of Him. As we start our first section let us recognize that we are unveiling His story. From the first verse in Genesis to the last in Revelation, all is about the Lord. To Him be the glory

***

God created one man Adam and his wife, Eve. They were to rule and subdue the earth together and multiply to fill it.

They enjoy a sinless existence in the presence of God. The garden in which the Lord had placed them was nothing less than paradise but there is one being in it that seeks to destroy their ideal life with God and take for himself what God has given to them. He is successful.

He deceives Eve into sinning but Adam makes the decision to sin on his own. Sin enters the perfect world and Adam and Eve die spiritually.

Thus starts God's plan of redemption.

From this point forward we read of God's commitment and work on behalf of all mankind to restore them to Himself. He will undo the work of the evil one and bring restoration to all who want it.

God promises to bless and redeem all and this is our story in this first section.

Chapter One

CREATION

And God Said...

In the beginning

God
Adam
Eve

Genesis 1, 2

The earth is formless and void
Seven days of Creation
Four Commands

There are arguments for and against how and when creation happened but we will just agree that God, in the beginning, created all things *ex nihilo* (out of nothing).

At this time the earth was *"formless and void."* Because the word "was" can also be translated as "became" it is possible that there is a gap or a major change that happened.

Some say that when satan (I deliberately never capitalize his name) rebelled it caused such a cataclysm in the universe that creation was devastated and became formless and void. Again, there can be arguments for and against this idea. For our study, we will only be looking at what God says about creation in the book of Genesis. We will leave the speculation of the how and when to others.

There are seven days in creation.

How long was a day for God? If we read the text literally we see *"and there was evening and there was morning one day."* We are going to read the text, therefore, as regular days and regular nights.

Some want to extend these days of creation into eons so that they can allow for evolution and other issues. One of these issues is that light travels at a set speed so how could it be that light from stars hundreds of millions of light years away could reach earth in but a day?

God is outside of His creation. He made the physical rules that govern that creation. I believe that if God can create out of nothing, including light and the physics to run that light, then He can place light anywhere He wants at any time He wants. Again, we will leave the discussion of physics and how it applies to creation to others.

And God said...

This phrase is repeated throughout the seven days of creation. Our God speaks and creation happens. Imagine the incredible power and wisdom it would take to create just a blade of grass from nothing let alone all of the universe. The power, wisdom, and creativity of God are evident as He speaks and the universes flies from His mouth.

Did He speak and the Big Bang happened? He does not tell us. But we do know that when He says, *"Let there be..."* whatever He desires comes into being.

All three persons of the Trinity are involved in creation.

God, the Father is who we usually think of when we read the creation story.

> *Praise him, sun and moon, praise him, all you shining stars. Praise him, you highest heavens and you waters above the skies. Let them praise the name of the LORD, For He commanded and they were created.*[1]

The Holy Spirit was also present and He is mentioned within the creation account.

---

1. Psalm 148:3

And the Spirit of God was moving over the surface of the waters.[2]

But, did you realize that the Son was also part of creation?

For by Him (Jesus) *all things were created, both in the heavens and on earth, visible and invisible, whether thrones or dominions or rulers or authorities, all things have been created by Him and for Him.*[3]

All of the person of God was present as He created time, and space and the universe, and all that it contains.

Creation becomes more complex as the days go by.

Simple	→	More Complex
Day 1 Light		Day 4 Specific Lights Seasons, Days Sun & Moon
Day 2 Air Water		Day 5 Flying Creatures Aquatic Animals
Day 3 Dry Land Plants		Day 6 Animal Life Adam ⟶ Eve

Day 1 – *and God said let there be light and there was light.*

Day 2 – God created the *"heavens."* This is not heaven as we think about it. Jewish thinking held three heavens. There is the heaven directly above, the heavens of the stars and God lived in the highest heaven, the one we usually associate with this word.

The heaven talked about here in day two is the air above the earth that at that time held a huge body of water in vapor form. Until the days of Noah this is how the earth was watered. On this day there is now water above and water below.

"And God saw that it was good."

---

2. Genesis 1:2

3. Colossians 1:16

Day 3 – God separates the oceans from dry land and creates all plant life. Here the phrase *"after their kind"* is used. All plants would reproduce themselves exactly as God made them. There is no evolution here as He says that *"they have their seed in them."* Each plant is complete as He created it.

"And God saw that it was good."

Day 4 – God expands on Day 1 by creating *"lights in the expanse of the heavens."* He creates seasons, days, years and the sun and moon for light on the earth. He sets the tilt of the earth, the distance of the sun and moon, and the magnetic field which are all part of God's wisdom in making life on earth possible.

"And God saw that it was good."

Day 5 – God expands His work from Day 2 by bringing life into the seas and into the air that He created. He creates all life in the water *"after their kind"* and all winged birds *"after its kind."* Again, no evolution needed. All were created as they are today and reproduce themselves as God made them to be.

"And God saw that it was good."

Day 6 – God expands His work from Day 3 by bringing life onto the dry land. He creates living creatures *"after their kind,"* cattle, creeping things and beasts of the earth *"after their kind,"* and everything that creeps on the ground *"after its kind."* Again, no room for evolution. All animals are created as they are and will reproduce themselves exactly as they were made.

"And God saw that it was good."

God also creates humans on the sixth day.[4]

Genesis 1:26 *Then God said, **"Let Us make man in Our image, according to Our likeness;** and <u>let them rule</u> over the fish of the sea and over the birds of the sky and over the cattle and over all the earth, and over every creeping thing that creeps on the earth." And God created man in His own image, in the image of God He created him; <u>male and female He created them.</u>" (emphasis mine)*

What does it mean to be made in the image of God? We were made differently than all other created things. The universe, the earth, the animals, birds, beasts, fish are not made in His image. Only humans, as male and female, are made like Him.

---

4. If you are interested in a detailed analysis of the creation of men and women then my book, "The Deception of Adam" is available at most online book stores.

And humans are made to be above the animals. We are not just another animal on the planet. We are not equal with other life on earth but are placed above all. God placed us as His representative in charge of the earth He had created.

Hebrews 2:8 *What is man, that Thou rememberest him? Or the son of man, that Thou art concerned about him? Thou hast made him for a little while lower than the angels; Thou hast crowned him with glory and honor, and hast appointed him over the works of Thy hands; Thou hast put all things in subjection under his feet." For in subjecting all things to him, He left nothing that is not subject to him."*

Crowned with "glory and honor" mankind was placed in charge of all that God had made.

Man and Woman.

At first, Adam was alone with God in a garden created for him. God commanded him to partake of everything in the garden except he was not to eat from *"the tree of the knowledge of good and evil."*

The Lord said that it was not good for the man to be alone and that he needed a suitable helper. His task of ruling in God's stead was too great for him to do alone. He brought every living creature to Adam to name and to realize his need for another like him.

It was then that God said that He would *"make a helper suitable for him."*

What is a "helper"?

Understanding the true meaning of the Hebrew word *"helper"* (ezer) requires a deeper historical and cultural perspective. It's important to recognize that words have evolved and taken on different meanings over time and across cultures. In order for us to understand how God uses a word, we need to go back to the original text.

"Helper" in modern times can suggest someone of lesser status, who assists with smaller tasks. Think employee, maid, someone with less skills, abilities, intelligence and resources available to do the less important work in order for the greater person to be enabled to accomplish their goals.

The Hebrew use of *"ezer"* (helper) paints a different picture.

Throughout the Old Testament, God Himself is referred to as our helper, *"Ezer"*, coming to our aid and offering assistance. This word conveys a sense of guidance and support from a leader, and one of greater power coming to give assistance to one in need. Here are God's usages of *"ezer"* concerning Himself:

Ps 121:1 I will lift up my eyes to the mountains; From where shall my help come?

Ps 121:2 <u>My help comes from the Lord</u> , Who made heaven and earth.

Ps 124:8 <u>Our help is in the name of the Lord</u> , Who made heaven and earth.

Ps 146:5 <u>How blessed is he whose help is the God of Jacob,</u> Whose hope is in the Lord his God,

Ps 20:2 <u>May He send you help from the sanctuary</u> And support you from Zion!

Ps 70:5 But I am afflicted and needy; Hasten to me, O God! <u>You are my help and my deliverer; O Lord</u> , do not delay.

Ps 89:19 Once You spoke in vision to Your godly ones, And said, "<u>I have given help to one who is mighty</u>; I have exalted one chosen from the people.

Ex 18:4 The other was named Eliezer, for he said, "<u>The God of my father was my help, and delivered me</u> from the sword of Pharaoh."

Ho 13:9 It is your destruction, O Israel, That you are against Me, against your help.

Dt 33:7 And this regarding Judah; so he said, "Hear, O Lord , the voice of Judah, And bring him to his people. With his hands he contended for them, And <u>may You be a help against his adversaries</u>."

Dt 33:29 "Blessed are you, O Israel; Who is like you, a people saved by the Lord, <u>Who is the shield of your help and the sword of your majesty! So your enemies will cringe before You</u>, And you will tread upon their high places."

The word *"ezer"* used in the Bible to describe God does not mean that He is subservient, weak, less intelligent or less capable. Instead, it means that God is stronger, more powerful, has more resources and is able to rescue and help us.

The *"ezer"* comes to one in need and is absolutely essential. Certainly God as *"ezer"* is not subservient or inferior like the maid that cleans up after us or the apprentice that hands the mechanic a tool. This word "helper" is used throughout the Old Testament to describe someone who is essential and more resourceful. God, as *"ezer"*, is not less than the one helped and neither is Eve.

We need one greater than ourselves, with more resources, intelligence, and power when we need help. So did Adam. Eve would be Adam's *"ezer"* in the same way that God is ours.

But, we have one more Hebrew word to look at – *"kenegdo"* which means "corresponding to" or "equal to." Your Bible might have this translated as "suitable."

We saw that the helper was one with greater resources coming to assist one in need. Here, through our second word, we now have the *"ezer kenegdo."* This second word further explains what a helper is in this context. Eve is a person equal to Adam. Together they are now able to "rule and subdue." Adam was not able to do this on his own but, now, with a helper equal to himself, they are equipped to do so.

God shows us that both Adam and Eve have equal resources. She was the right hand to his left. Both are necessary to carry out God's will.

She was not the the superior helper as God is to us but the equal of Adam. Neither was to be superior to the other. Eve is like Adam, equal to him and is his counterpart. Neither are superior. Neither is subordinate. There is no hierarchy instituted by God.

God had showed Adam his need to have someone like him and then brought Eve to him to be his counterpart and completion in serving the Lord.

Eve is made from the flesh of Adam and he immediately recognizes that she is *"flesh of my flesh."* Finally, here was someone corresponding to him.

God's original design is one man and one woman reproducing themselves in His image. The first relationship we see is marriage and marriage as He intended it to be.

"God saw all that He had made, and, behold, it was very good."

Adam and Eve were given four commands.

Genesis 1:28 *And God blessed them; and God said to them, "Be fruitful and multiply, and fill the earth, and subdue it; and rule over the fish of the sea and over the birds of the sky, and over every living thing that moves on the earth."*

Three commands He gave to Adam and Eve together.

- Be fruitful – multiplying and filling the earth

- Subdue the earth

- Rule over the earth

One command He gave to Adam before He created Eve.

- Do not eat from the tree of life

In six days God created all that exists in the physical world!

That He created the earth at all is astonishing but look at the diversity. He could have made one or only a few kinds of fish and birds, mammals and reptiles, flowers and trees but He made thousands. We are still discovering plants, fish and animals that He created. In the universe, the sun, moon and a few stars would have been impressive but we are only now finding tens of thousands of galaxies each with millions of stars.

And God rested from all His work.

Genesis 2:1 *Thus the heavens and the earth were completed, and all their hosts. And by the seventh day God completed His work which He had done; and He rested on the seventh day from all His work which He had done. Then God blessed the seventh day and sanctified it, because in it He rested from all His work which God had created and made.*

What can we say about our God? Words fail to express His magnitude and magnificence.

Chapter Two

CONSEQUENCES

A Choice to Obey or Disobey

God
Adam
Eve
Serpent

Genesis 3

Temptation by the serpent
Sin of Adam and Eve
Curses and consequences
Promised Savior

G od had created Adam and Eve and provided all of their needs and had made only one requirement for them – obedience. Otherwise, the world was theirs.

He had made them master of this wonderful place and withheld only one tree. This tree was representative of the opportunity to walk with God or reject Him. They were offered life or death depending on whether they obeyed.

Adam and Eve lived in this garden the Lord had made for them but they were not alone. The serpent was also present.

Adam and Eve had been given authority over the earth. Satan, who had once had an honored position serving the Lord, wanted that authority. He also wanted to destroy them and their relationship with God.

Adam and Eve, having no knowledge of evil, could not comprehend hatred and deception and one who would have in his heart the desire to hurt them. So, when the serpent approaches Eve she innocently speaks with him.

The Accusation

- Satan starts the conversation with Eve by <u>questioning the Word of God</u> – *"Did God really say?"*

- Then he <u>changes the Word of God</u> – *"that you shall not eat from **any** tree?"* God had given them permission to eat from every tree but one - the serpent is twisting the Word.

- Eve responds but she makes the mistake of <u>adding to the Word of God</u> – *"you shall not eat from it **or touch it.**"* God hadn't said they couldn't touch the tree but she had not been there when God gave the command to Adam so she had not heard it firsthand.

Now that the serpent has changed and distorted what God has said he is ready to malign His character and set forth his temptation.

He accuses God of being a liar

- Satan tells her that God has not told her the truth. *"You shall not surely die!"*

He accuses God of not being good and offers a temptation

- He is holding out on you. *"For God knows that in the day you eat from it your eyes will be opened and you will be like God knowing good and evil."*

The temptation works

Satan's deception has worked. The serpent has tempted Eve to <u>see God differently</u>. God is not who He says that He is and, therefore, she cannot trust Him.

She believes the serpent and now when she looks at the tree she <u>sees it differently</u>. She sees that:

- *"the tree was good for food"* (lust of the flesh)

- *"It was a delight to the eyes"* (lust of the eyes)

- "desirable to make one wise" (boastful pride of life)[1]

Sin enters the world

"She took from its fruit and ate; and she gave also to <u>her husband with her</u>, and he ate."

Although Eve was deceived by the serpent Adam remained silent. He was right there with her and said nothing.

Scripture tells us that Adam was not deceived but willingly chose to disobey anyway. The fall of humanity is placed upon his shoulders, not Eve's, for his sin was intentional. Eve had been tricked but Adam knew what he was doing when he ate the fruit. He made the decision to disobey God.

Together they have chosen, whether deceived or not, to sin.

In this one action they:

- Disobeyed the word of God

- Didn't believe the word of God

- Placed their will above God's

This is high treason against the ruler of the universe. Sin has entered Adam and Eve and the world changes.

Immediate effects of sin

Shame – they covered themselves with fig leaves whereas before they had been *"naked and unashamed."*

Ruined their relationship with God – they hid from Him

Distorted thinking – thought they could hide from God

Blame – Adam blamed the woman and God. Eve blamed the serpent.

When confronted by God, Eve speaks about what actually happened. *"The serpent deceived me, and I ate."*[2]

---

1. 1 John 2:16

2. Genesis 3:13

She neither tries to defend herself or blame anyone else for her actions. She could have said, "Adam was with me and stayed silent. It's his fault." Instead, she realizes that she had been deceived and admits it.

When Adam is confronted the tone is much different.

> *"The <u>woman</u> whom <u>You</u> gave to be with me, she gave me from the tree, and I ate."* (emphasis mine) [3]

Adam attributes his sin to Eve and to God for bringing her to him rather than take responsibility for his decisions.

God brings curses and consequences for their sin

<u>Satan is cursed</u>

> *"The Lord God said to the serpent, 'BECAUSE YOU have done this, <u>Cursed are you</u>..." (emphasis mine)*[4]

<u>The earth is cursed because of Adam</u> - thorns and thistles now grow and animals become fearful of man. His work has changed to hard toil and sweat.

> *"Then to Adam He said, 'BECAUSE YOU have listened to the voice of your wife and have eaten from the tree about which I commanded you saying, 'You shall not eat from it; <u>Cursed is the ground BECAUSE OF YOU</u>"* (emphasis mine)[5]

<u>Physical death</u>. God had told Adam that *"in the day that you eat from it you shall surely die."* Although they still lived physically they would now die and return to the dust from which God made them.

---

3. Genesis 3:12

4. Genesis 3:14 NASB

5. Genesis 3:17 NASB

> *"You are dust, and to dust you shall return."* [6]

Death has entered the world.

<u>Spiritual death</u>. They died spiritually and all of their offspring are born dead in sin.

> *"...through one man sin entered into the world, and death through sin, and so death spread to all mankind, because all sinned..."* [7]

<u>Relationship distorted</u>. Eve did not go to her husband when she was tempted. Now, because of the fall she would desire him but he would be a despot over her.

> *"Your desire will be for your husband but he shall rule over you."* [8]

What does "desire" mean?

We must go to the Word to accurately understand the significance of this word, rather than relying on our own subjective interpretation.

There are only three instances where this word is used in Scripture.

1. *"To the woman He said, 'I will greatly multiply Your pain in childbirth, In pain you will bring forth children; Yet your **desire** will be for your husband, but he will rule over you.'"* Ge 3:16

2. *"If you do well, will not your countenance be lifted up? And if you do not do well, sin is crouching at the door; and its **desire** is for you, but you must master it."* Ge 4:7

3. *"I am my beloved's, and his **desire** is for me."* So 7:10

The Theological Wordbook of the Old Testament will shed some light on this word:

---

6. Genesis 3:19 NASB

7. Romans 5:12-21 NASB

8. Genesis 3:16

Tesuqa - desire, longing. This noun appears only three times in the OT, once in Song 7:10. The woman says of her beloved: "I am my beloved's and his 'desire' is for me." The two remaining references are Gen 3:16 and 4:7. In the latter passage God is speaking to Cain and says to him that sin is like a crouching beast "hungering, intent upon" Cain. In the former passage God says, "Your 'desire' shall be to your husband but he shall rule over you." This is obviously neither an intensification nor a warping of a pre-existing hierarchy between the sexes for no such hierarchy is alluded to. There are two differences between the Gen passage (3:16) and that in the Song of Solomon. In the former the reference is to the wife's desire for her husband. In the latter it is the bride-groom's desire for the bride. Second, in the Gen passage the reference to "desire" is in a context of sin and judgment. In the latter, the reference is in a context of joy and love. [9]

Many people have interpreted this passage in Genesis as Eve wanting to take control and dominate Adam. However, looking at the word usage in Scripture, this interpretation is not accurate, and it only serves to push a specific paradigm into Scripture.

The word used in the passage simply describes a longing or desire - it does not indicate any kind of need for power or authority.

Your desire and his rule

Some see this desire/rule as God's new mandate for humans. Eve is to be inferior and Adam superior. Eve is to be ruled, contained, and dominated from now on.

The idea that God intended for Adam to rule over Eve and keep her under his control is not supported by the original language of the text. In fact, the specific word used to describe Adam's "authority" over Eve after the Fall is not the same one used in the creation story.

Let's look at "rule over."

The word we translate as "rule" used <u>after the fall</u> in Genesis 3:16 is not the same word God used when He told Adam and Eve to "rule" and subdue every living thing <u>before the fall</u> in Genesis 1:26.

Had God intended the same meaning, He would have used the same word in both verses.

---

9. Hamilton, V. P. (1999). 2352 .□□□□In R. L. Harris, G. L. Archer Jr., & B. K. Waltke (Eds.), Theological Wordbook of the Old Testament (electronic ed., p. 913). Moody Press.

Here is the first usage of "rule" in 1:26:

> radah; a prim. root; to have dominion, rule, dominate:—dominated(1), had dominion(1), have dominion(1), prevailed(1), rule(12), ruled(4), ruling(1), subdued(1), subdues(1).

God gave Adam **and** Eve a rightful dominion over His creation and used this word to describe His intentions.

Here is the second usage of "rule" in 3:16. It is a different Hebrew word.

> mashal (605c); a prim. root; to rule, have dominion, reign:-dominion(1), gain control(1), govern(1), had charge(1), have authority(1), master(1), obtain dominion(1), really going to rule(1), rule(27), ruled(5), ruler(18), ruler's(2), rulers(6), rules(9), ruling(3), wielded(1)

The first usage, "*radah* – rule," does not have the meaning of to "gain control" because God had already given it to Adam and Eve. It does not "obtain dominion" for it was endowed by Him.

It is only the second word that shows a usurpation of control in order to rule in a way that God did not ordain.

Eve's desire was for her husband but he is going to "*mashal*" – gain control, take charge and authority, have dominion over and "really going to rule" her.

With this understanding, the verse could be translated, *"Your desire shall be for your husband BUT he will instead dominate you."*

Eve did not turn to "her husband with her" when the serpent spoke to her

Eve missed an opportunity to seek guidance from her husband, Adam, when the serpent tempted her with the forbidden fruit. How could she know about evil, that he sought to "steal, kill and destroy" them? Her innocence gave her no reason to suspect or distrust. This tragic event broke the once perfect oneness between Adam and Eve, resulting in a satan-inspired and sin-filled distance between them.

Eve now yearns to reconnect with Adam and restore their once harmonious union. However, their relationship has taken a turn for the worse. She "desires" to be united with him as they were before BUT his heart has changed toward her.

Adam now sees himself as superior to her and assumes the role of a tyrant, rather than an equal partner.

No longer does he sees his "helper" as one that is equal and corresponding to him. Now, he has blamed her for his own sin and placed himself above her. In my book, "The Deception of Adam," I write a full explanation of how that blame has not only divided men and women but has been carried out throughout the ages and into the church. The evil one continues to deceive us about God's original design.

<u>Pain in childbirth.</u> God would *"greatly multiply your pain in childbirth."*

Eve's consequence was physical like Adam's. His consequence regarded work that would now be a hardship and Eve's was that bringing forth children would be hard and painful. But...

Hope of a Savior.

God had known that this day would come before He created the universe and He already had a plan for salvation.

Even though Eve had been deceived, He tells her that He will bring a Savior through her. Her sin was not intentional as was Adam's.

> "And I will put enmity between you *(serpent)* and the woman and between your (serpent's) seed and her seed"[10] *(emphasis mine)*

Here is the first promise of a Savior. God tells of a prolonged struggle with wounds on both sides but eventual victory of her seed. This is the first gospel.

In the Old Testament we see the record of the *"enmity between you and the woman and between her seed and your seed"* and then in the New Testament we will see the coming of the promised Savior (her seed) and His stepping on the head of the evil one in victory.

---

10. Genesis 3:15

This promised Savior is the theme of all 66 books of the Bible and this is His story.

Faith and an exit.

Adam calls the woman "Eve" which means "life." This shows that he has believed in God's promise of the coming Savior.

The Lord clothes the man and woman, covering their shame and showing that He still cares for them. Then in His mercy and grace He makes them leave the garden.

Because they know evil if they were to eat of the fruit of the tree of life now they would stay in their fallen state forever. So, God sends them from the garden and guards it against their return.[11]

The rest of our Bible focuses on building a people through whom the promised Savior will come.

---

11. Some of this chapter was taken from my book, "The Deception of Adam."

Chapter Three

CORRUPTION

The Journey to Salvation

Adam
Eve
Cain
Able
Seth
Enoch
Noah

Genesis 4-8

God sees the corruption on the earth
Noah is instructed to build an ark
The flood covers the earth

After the Garden

Adam and Eve began to have children and fill the earth. Their first son was Cain. He is the first murderer. The knowledge of good and evil that they acquired has been passed to their son who takes the knowledge of evil to its logical end – death.

Cain was jealous of his brother Abel and his relationship with God. Abel's heart was for God but Cain made his sacrifice to God not out of love for God but because he was supposed to. You could say that his offering is the first instance of religion.

God rejected Cain's religion but accepts Abel's relationship. It is the heart, not the actions, that God looks upon.

The Lord tells Cain that he need not feel down for if he does well things will be well for him but reminds him that sin desires him and that he must master it. That is the same for us today. But, Cain allows sin to be his master and kills his brother.

Cain had been a farmer but because of his actions God curses the ground for him. No longer will he be able to grow crops. But God says that He will protect Him from others that might want to hurt him thus showing His mercy and His heart toward him.

Cain goes on to have many wives and many children. His descendants were people of architecture, weaving, manufacture, poetry and music. They also practiced polygamy, had great pride and did not worship God.

Adam and Eve had many children over the course of their 900 plus years. One of those children born to them was Seth. Seth, and his descendants, followed the Lord and one of those descendants was Noah.

Corruption of the line of Seth

The descendants of Cain, who did not worship God, began to intermarry with the descendants of Seth who did. This had disastrous results as it always does when believers and unbelievers come together.

First, God shortened the lifespan of mankind from the normal over 900 years to 120. *"Then the Lord saw that the wickedness of man was great on the earth, and that **every intent** of the thoughts of his hearts was **only evil continually**."*[1]

Corruption happens when followers of the Lord allow themselves to be absorbed by the godless.

There had been thousands of years since Seth and the corruption between his line and the line of Cain had almost been complete. In the midst of an entire planet that had been corrupted by sin, God finds one man who still walks with Him. Only one man remained faithful.

> *The Lord said, 'I will blot out man whom I have created from the face of the land, from man to animals to creeping things and to birds of the sky'...Now the earth was corrupt in the sight of God, and the earth was filled with violence. God looked on the earth and behold, it was corrupt; for all flesh*

---

1. Genesis 6:5

had corrupted their way upon the earth. **"But, Noah found favor in the eyes of the Lord.** *Noah was a righteous man, blameless in his time; Noah walked with God."*[2]

The Flood cleanses the earth

The sin that started in the garden has blossomed into full blown corruption and God will cleanse the earth and start over.

He tells Noah of His plans of destruction but also of hope and restoration.

Noah is given detailed plans of a huge ship he is to build that will hold him, his family, and representatives of all animal life on earth. God will destroy all life on earth but He says that He will then establish His covenant with Noah.

Noah is to partner with God in His plan of renewal. He will care for the living things of the earth on his ship during the flood so that they can be released again to repopulate the earth.

Thus Noah did; according to all that God had commanded him, so he did.[3]

The ark Noah builds with his sons is estimated to be able to hold some 45,000 sheep-sized animals and there would still be the size of 104 railroad cars available for storage, living and range room for the animals. God brought the animals of the earth to the ark and closed the door.

Noah was 600 years old when the floods came. His sons and wives came into the ark with him. Once the flood starts, Noah and his family will be in the ark for 224 days.

The water that was suspended above fell

Until this time it had never rained on the earth. The Lord had watered the earth with a mist from the waters held above since the first day of Creation.

Now, *"the floodgates of the sky were opened."* And water came from underneath the earth as well. *"The fountains of the great deep burst open."* The rain fell for forty days and forty nights.

---

2. Genesis 6:12

3. Genesis 6:22

"The water prevailed…the water prevailed…the water prevailed" until even the highest mountains were covered with water. Noah, his family, and the animals of the earth floated on the water above all that were no more.

God sent a wind, closed the floodgates of water from the deep and from the sky and the water started to recede. And they waited.

They waited for land to appear, for God to provide, for a new start. I can only imagine the grief they might feel knowing that all life on earth had perished except what was left on the ark.   I can only imagine the anxious waiting for dry land and what their life might be like after this. They waited for God to tell them it was time to start over.

The ark empties

The animals go out *"by their families"* to *"breed abundantly on the earth and be fruitful and multiply."* Noah builds an altar and offers a sacrifice to the God Who has saved them.

Lessons from the ark

Noah was *"blameless in his time."* This means that even though all around him were corrupt he could still walk with God. He did not allow himself and his family to be absorbed into the culture of wickedness around him.

For us, this means that we are without excuse if we do not follow God as we walk in our corrupt culture.

"Noah did all according to what the Lord had commanded him." What God had asked Him to do may have made him the laughing stock of his time. One reason would be that Noah told them that water would fall from the sky. That was something that had never happened before. Noah sounded insane. Nevertheless, Noah would believe and obey God above the world.

We can do the same today.

"I will establish My covenant with you – and you shall enter the ark – you and your sons, and your wife, and your sons' wives with you." Noah was righteous and God blessed him AND his family because of it.

Our actions or inactions also effect those we love.

Immediately after leaving the ark Noah worshipped God. I'm sure there was a lot to do in this new life but the first priority for Noah was to worship God and give thanks for his salvation and that of his family.

Every day we can worship and give thanks for our Lord has saved us out of the corruption of the world to new life with Him.

Chapter Four

CONFUSION

Covenant, Repopulation, Rebellion and the Sons of Noah

Noah
Ham
Shem
Japheth

Genesis 8:20-11:9

Covenant with Noah
Tower of Babel
Confusion of languages
Scattering over the earth
Beginning of the nations

Noah and his family left the ark, worshiped the Lord and now God makes a covenant with Noah.

From this time forward *"while the earth remains, seedtime and harvest, cold and heat, summer and winter, day and night shall not cease."* [1]

---

1. Genesis 8:22

God establishes a covenant with Noah and all his descendants and every living creature on the earth never to destroy the earth with a flood again. And the sign of this covenant is the rainbow He places in the sky. Most likely, there had never been a rainbow before this time. Imagine seeing a sign such as this appear in the sky.

And God institutes a new way to live

He changes their relationship with animals – animals will now fear man.

He changes their diet – they can now eat meat except not with the blood in it.

He initiates human government - people are responsible to govern themselves.

He renews a partial command to "*be fruitful and multiply and fill the earth.*"

This is almost the same command that the Lord had given to Adam and Eve. What is missing is to "*rule and subdue the earth.*" They no longer rule as God's representatives as the evil one is now prince of this world.

The sons of Noah

From the three sons of Noah, Shem, Ham and Japheth, come all people on earth. We can all trace our lineage back to them.

From the line of Shem the Savior would come. From the line of Japheth would come the Gentiles. From the line of Ham came those of Ethiopia, Egypt, Put, and Canaan.

Noah built a vineyard and partook too deeply of its fruit becoming drunk and exposing himself in his tent. Ham, the father of Canaan, gossiped to his brothers about his father rather than covering him up and caring for him. His brothers placed a garment, and without looking, placed it over their father's nakedness. Ham's son, Canaan, is cursed for his father's behavior.

What had Ham done wrong? Ham had dishonored his father. Because Ham dishonored his father, Noah wishes upon him a son who would do the same.

He prophesied that the descendants of Ham (Canaanites) would be servants to his brothers' offspring. He says that Shem will be blessed by the LORD and that spiritual blessings will come to the descendants of Japheth (Gentiles) through that blessing. He asks that God would enlarge Japheth's territory.

Noah's prophecy comes true.

Rebellion against God

Chapter 10 of Genesis tells of all the descendants of the sons of Noah and where they expanded. Whole peoples came from them and they filled the known earth. They also used the same language.

The Lord had told them after they came from the ark to *"populate the earth abundantly and multiply in it."* They are about to disobey that command.

As people expanded eastward they decided not to scatter over the earth but to create a city with a tower – a marker of their determination to live as they pleased apart from God's command. So, they started to build the tower *"whose top would reach into heaven."*

They said that they wanted to *"make for themselves a name otherwise we will be scattered abroad over the face of the whole earth."* They were actively and intentionally defying God.

The Lord, in His mercy, would limit their ability to disobey Him.

God's limitation of sin

> *"Come, let Us go down and there confuse their language, that they may not understand one another's speech."[2]*

I have often thought of the great amount of evil that could be done if we did not have to sleep. Those extra eight hours could be used for great damage. In the same way, one people with the same language could also create great evil.

> *"And the LORD said, "Behold, they are one people, and they all have the same language. And this is what they began to do, and now nothing which they purpose to do will be impossible for them."[3]*

So, the Lord created many languages and those who understood one another gathered together and God *"scattered them abroad over the whole face of the earth."* They had set their will against God's but He would not allow them to succeed.

"And they stopped building the city."

The descendants of Japheth went to the west and to the north. Ham's descendants moved to the south and west and Shem's moved toward the south and east. Now, the Lord will

---

2. Genesis 11:7

3. Genesis 11:6

work through the line of Shem to create a people for Himself and through whom He would bring the Savior.

I wonder if the push toward a one world government today that is seen in Revelation is the world system trying to come back together to oppose the will of God.

COVENANT

The Father of Many Nations

2000 - 1600 BC

Genesis 11:31-50:26

Abraham
Sarah
Hagar
Ishmael
Lot
Isaac
Rebekah
Esau

Jacob
Laban
Leah
Rachel
Twelve sons
Pharaoh
Joseph's sons

Abrahamic covenant
Isaac, the son of promise
Jacob and his twelve brothers
Joseph, the deliverer

God had promised a redeemer back in Genesis 3:15. He has grown mankind, cleansed them, scattered them and is now focused in on the line of Shem as He continues His promise of a Savior to come.

From Adam to Noah to Shem comes Abram. He lives in the land of Ur which is a fairly pagan area at the time. He is married to Sarai. His father moves them to Haran and they stay there until he dies. Then he hears the Lord's call.

The Abrahamic Covenant

God calls to Abram and tells him to leave his life behind and go to a land God would show him. Abram sets out not knowing where he will end up but trusting God to take him there.

Abram is 75 years old but God makes a covenant with him. He tells him that a great nation will come from him. Abram currently had no children and the likelihood of him having children when he wife was also aged seemed impossible.

The Lord says that He will provide Abram with a land but he does not know where. And God says that He will bless Abram making his name great and that all nations of the world will be blessed by him.

"So Abram went forth as the LORD has spoken to him."[1]

Understanding this covenant is absolutely essential to understand the rest of Scripture.

Everything after this point falls under this covenant. There will be other covenants to come but they will also be under the Abrahamic Covenant.

Your understanding of the national, personal and universal promises are also needed in order to be able to grasp the whole of the Biblical story.

ABRAHAMIC COVENANT
Genesis 12:1-3; 15

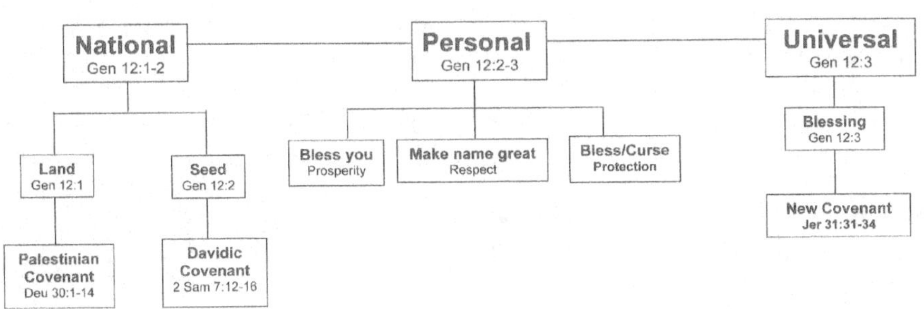

I will bless you, And make your name great; And so you shall be a blessing; And I will bless those who bless you, And the one who curses you I will curse. And in you all the families of the earth shall be blessed.

---

1. Genesis 12:4

God will make a nation of Abram

1) He will give him descendants (**seed**) and,

2) He will give him a place for them to live (**land**). In addition, God promises him

3) personal blessings and curses for those who become his enemy.

Through Abram all nations will be **blessed** because the Savior will come through him.

Abram's decision to leave his land and go with God was based on faith. It had to be because everything that God was promising seemed impossible at his age and status. But Abram believed God and He set out for a land that He did not know but with a God in whom He believed.

Unilateral, Unconditional and Eternal

In Genesis 15 God meets with Abram again and restates the covenant. Abram questions God because he has no child to carry on his name let alone become a nation.

God tells Abram to look at the stars and says that his offspring will be as many. *"Then he believed in the LORD; and He reckoned it to him as righteousness."* Abram's faith, as ours today, is the basis for our righteousness before God.

God seals the covenant by passing alone between the sacrifice Abram had prepared. That only God passed between the pieces shows that its fulfillment is only God's responsibility and that Abram did not agree to do anything to bring it about. In chapter 17 the LORD tells Abram that the covenant is eternal and to all his descendants.

God changes Abram's name to Abraham which means "father of many" and Sarai's name to Sarah which meant "princess" and told him that his aged wife would bear him a son.

Now, God asks them to participate in a sign of the covenant. All males over eight days old are to be circumcised. This would be a daily reminder to them that they were chosen by God and belonged to Him.

The son by the will of man

Sarah had been barren and this was shameful in her culture. She knew the promise of God but still she did not become pregnant. As we often do, she decided to hurry God's will. And is always the case when we do not wait on God there are consequences.

Sarah persuaded Abraham to sleep with her maid, Hagar. She blamed God for preventing her from having children but thought that she could have a child through her maid servant. Abraham listened to his wife but there is no record of him going to the Lord for confirmation that this was how God wished to bring about His promise to Abram.

Hagar conceived and after she did she showed contempt for her mistress. Sarah in turn treated her harshly and Hagar ran away.

The angel of the Lord appeared to her and told her to return and submit and that God would greatly multiply her descendants. He told her she would have a son and to call him Ishmael, that he would be wild and oppositional and that everyone would be against him.

The son of promise

Sarah does become pregnant when she is ninety-nine years old. God waited until she was far beyond childbearing age to show that it was He that made this happen.

God tells Abraham that the child's name will be Isaac and that God would establish His covenant with him.

Ishmael has lost his place of honor and mocks Isaac. Sarah pushed Abraham to send Hagar and her son away and he does.

Isaac would become the father of the Jews and Ishmael the father of Arabs. The conflict that started between these two children continues to this day. The son of promise is in conflict with the son of man's will.

The testing of Abraham and Isaac.

The son of Abraham's heart may have become an idol, for God asks him to sacrifice Isaac to Him. Hadn't God promised a countless number of descendants would come through Isaac? How could that be if Isaac dies? But, Abraham rose early and took Isaac to a place God led him to sacrifice him as commanded.

He and Isaac would leave the servants, *"go over there, worship and return to you."* Abraham and Isaac built the altar and he bound his son and placed him on it. As Abraham stretched out his hand to slay his son the angel of the Lord stopped him.

What do we make of this?

Hebrews 11:17 *By faith Abraham, when he was tested, offered up Isaac; and he who had received the promises was offering up his only begotten son; it was he to whom it was said, "In Isaac your descendants shall be called." He considered that God is able to raise men even from the dead; from which he also received him back as a symbol.*

Faith. Because God had promised, Abraham reasoned that He would raise Isaac from the dead if needed to fulfill His promises. But this event is as much about Isaac as it was about Abraham.

Isaac would have been at least a teenager by now so he most certainly could have gotten away from his old father but he did not. He allowed himself to be placed on the altar for sacrifice.

What I see in this passage is the faith of Abraham but also the faith of Isaac in the promises of God and submission to His will.

Jacob

Isaac grew and married Rebekah and he had two sons – twins – and they struggled within her. God told her that two nations were growing inside of her and that the first born would serve the younger.

Esau, the older, was a hunter but Jacob was peaceful. Isaac favored Esau and Rebekah favored Jacob.

As the older, Esau would be assured a double portion of Isaac's estate but he could lose it for serious sin or trade it away. One day, while very hungry he did just that. He wanted stew that Jacob made and traded his spiritual heritage to Jacob for a bowl of it.

Now, Jacob wanted Isaac's blessing too. By deception he gets it.

By tricking his blind father while his brother is not there he gets Isaac to give him irreversible legal blessing. Two times he has tricked his brother taking away his birthright and now his blessing. Esau swore to kill his brother so Jacob fled.

Now Jacob is the one who is tricked. He loves Rachel but is tricked by her father into marrying her sister. He married Leah and then was able to also marry Rachael and lived with, and worked for, her father Laban.

Jacob didn't love Leah so mercifully God allowed her to have children. Rachel seemed to be barren so she talked him into sleeping with her maid in order to get children in the same way Sarah had done to Abraham.

Leah stopped getting pregnant so she pushed Jacob to sleep with her maid to get more children. Eventually Rachael has two sons, Joseph and Benjamin. In total Jacob ends up with 12 sons by four women.

Joseph

Rachel died giving birth to Benjamin. Jacob's beloved was gone and so he favored their two sons. The other ten brothers were jealous of them.

Joseph told on his brothers and they despised him more. Jacob made Joseph a wonderful coat and he went to his brothers to tell them of dreams he had where they bowed down to him. That made them hate him even more.

One day Jacob sent Joseph to check on his brother while wearing his many colored coat. His brothers had had enough of him and they decided to get rid of him. They sold him to passing slave traders and put blood on his coat. They brought the coat to their father saying they had found it and implying that Joseph must have been killed.

Joseph was sold to an Egyptian officer of Pharaoh. *"The Lord was with Joseph so he became a successful man."*[2] But he is falsely accused and is sent to prison.

While in prison the Lord was still with Joseph and gave him favor in that place. One day he rightly interprets the dreams of two prisoners, one of which ends up working for Pharaoh.

Pharaoh has a disturbing dream that no one can interpret and this man remembers Joseph. Joseph is brought before Pharaoh and gives the interpretation telling him that his dream tells of coming famine after seven years of plenty. Pharaoh is impressed and puts Joseph in charge in Egypt and only Pharaoh had more power.

In one day, after years in prison, Joseph has become the second most powerful man in Egypt. He is given a wife and goes about organizing the country to store grain for the coming famine.

Deliverance and protection

The famine spreads just as Joseph said and reaches his family of origin. They must go to Egypt now to purchase food.

They do not know that Joseph is there let alone that he is powerful. It has been many years since they have seen him and when they come before him they do not recognize him in his Egyptian clothing. They bow before him just as they did in Joseph's dream.

Joseph is able to save his family from starvation and when Pharaoh finds out about them he has them all move to Egypt to be safe and protected.

The boy they sent away had become their deliverer. God had been with Joseph so that this day of deliverance could come. What his brothers meant for evil against him God meant for good for all people.

---

2. Genesis 39:2

From Adam to Abraham

Everything is in place for the promised seed of the woman to come through the line of Abraham. Out of all the peoples on earth God has chosen Abraham and from him He will grow a nation and bring a Savior for all mankind.

We finish this section with the Abrahamic covenant in place and directing the future. Other covenants will be added under this covenant bringing greater depth and information on how to live before God.

We leave the book of Genesis. The foundation has been laid and we will see God build upon it.

Section 2 – A Family to a Nation

God is working out His plan of salvation

He has gone from the garden with Adam and Eve to moving the family of Jacob, now called "Israel" to Egypt where He will now grow this family of promise into a nation.

This "seed" will be given a "land" and they and all who support them will receive "blessings" and nations that oppose them will receive "curses."

Land, seed, blessing. This is the Abrahamic Covenant. Keep it in mind as we move forward.

Chapter Six

CAPTIVITY 1

From Guests to Captives

1590 - 1440 BC

Pharaoh
Pharaoh's daughter
Moses
Aaron

Exodus 1-15
Psalm 105

Oppression and slavery
Birth, education and flight of Moses
The burning bush
The ten plagues
Exodus from Egypt

God led the family to Egypt. Why?

Egypt was a place of safety for the people of Israel. The Egyptians would not intermarry with anyone outside of themselves. They would not live among the Egyptians but beside them. This meant that God could grow this family into a nation in a place where they would stay a people.

Unlike the line of Seth who was corrupted because of their living with their ungodly neighbors, the people would stay separate and uncorrupted.

And grow they did. From a large family of about 100 people they grew to a nation of two million in only 200 years.

The new Pharaoh grew afraid of these people. He had not known Joseph who had saved Egypt and all the world around it from starvation. To him this huge nation among them would continue to multiply and rise up against Egypt and conquer it so he turned them into slaves to control them.

But even under great oppression God continued to grow this people.

The Egyptians in response made their lives even more bitter with hard labor. Then they instructed the midwives to kill all newborn male children. But the midwives feared God and disobeyed. Then Pharaoh commanded that all newborn males be thrown into the Nile.

Moses

Into this environment Moses was born. As he was a male baby, his birth was kept hidden until he grew too big.

His mother placed him in a basket and set it in the Nile relinquishing him to the Lord's care. She had given his life and future into the hands of God and His will would be done. His sister, Miriam, watched from a distance to see what would happen.

God sent the daughter of Pharaoh to find him floating on the water. When Miriam saw that she had pity on the baby she asked if she should go and find a nursemaid for him. Of course she went and got her mother.

So, Moses' mother was paid to raise him until he was weaned, which would have been several years, and then he went to live at the palace. He would have had an educated and privileged life but he was still of the people of Israel and he would have to decide which culture he would ultimately adopt.

He made the decision. One day he defended a Hebrew that was being beaten and he killed the Egyptian doing it. The event was seen and he fled Egypt to save his life.

He came upon a well in Midian and saw shepherds treating seven sisters harshly. Again, Moses came to the rescue and drove them away and then drew the water for them himself. The women's father gave Moses his daughter in marriage and he began his life there.

Forty years later the angel of the Lord appeared to him in a burning bush that was not consumed by the fire.

"I am the God of your father, the God of Abraham, the God of Isaac, and the God of Jacob." [1]

God introduced Himself as the God of the covenant with Abraham that had passed to Isaac and to Jacob. He was also the God of Moses and the people held captive in Egypt. God was about to deliver them and He would do it through Moses.

Moses was not thrilled about this idea. First, he was wanted in Egypt for murder. Next, his people were slaves of a powerful empire. He complains and offers a series of questions that were really his attempt at trying to escape God's will for him.

But God is not deterred. Moses will go. He will speak with Pharaoh. He will bring God's people out of Egypt. And he is to tell the people that "I AM" had sent him.

"I AM WHO I AM." This is the name God gave to Moses for Himself.

This name is used in relation to creation, His holiness, redemption, self-existence and His dynamic presence. I AM. If you think about it this is an astonishing name.

It is not, "I was," or "I will be" but an ever unchanging, powerful present. It is not a name that describes but a statement of self-existence. *YHWH – I AM.*

When this name is translated in the Bible you will see LORD in all capitals. I AM was with Moses and would go with him in all of His power to Egypt. I AM is with you right now.

Out of Egypt

God allowed Moses to take his brother Aaron to speak for him due to his begging God not to send him. God would go with them, teach them what to say and do, and gave Moses a staff through which God would perform signs and miracles.

Most of us know the story of Moses before Pharaoh and the ten plagues that finally convinced Pharaoh to release the people. You may not know that each of the plagues refuted a "god" of Egypt.

10 PLAGUES AND THE CORRESPONDING
DEFEATED EGYPTIAN "GOD"

PLAGUE	"GOD"
Water Turned to Blood	Hapi
Frogs Coming From the Nile	Heket
Lice From the Earth's Dust	Geb
Swarms of Flies	Khepri
Death of Cattle and Livestock	Hathor
Ashes Turned to Boils and Sores	Isis
Hail in the Form of Fire	Nut
Locus Sent From the Sky	Seth
Three Days of Complete Darkness	Ra
Death of the Firstborn	Osiris

One by one God showed their gods to be nothing and Himself to be the true God. The last plague defeating their god, Osiris – giver of life, took the life of all first born in Egypt. God warned the Hebrews that this death of the firstborn was coming. Each family was to kill an unblemished lamb and place some of the blood on the doorframe as a covering.

This was the first Passover. The Lord would "pass over" all houses that had the blood on the door frame and their first born would be spared. This is a symbol of Christ, our Passover lamb. His death in our place saves us.

Pharaoh's first born son died and he finally relents and sends the Hebrews out of Egypt. They are allowed to take silver, gold and clothing from the Egyptians on their way out.

God led the nation and their flocks out of Egypt by a pillar of fire at night and a pillar of cloud by day.

Pharaoh's heart was hardened and he determined to come after the Hebrews and the people are frightened when they see him and his army coming for them. But the Lord was their defense.

The pillar of cloud moved behind the people to be between them and the army. Then Moses stretched out his hand and God swept back the waters of the Red Seas so that dry land appeared through the middle.

The people passed through safely. The army came after them and when they were in the midst of the sea God had Moses stretch his hand over the waters and this time the waters returned drowning the army that sought to destroy them.

The family became a nation in their time in Egypt and now this nation was on the move to a land God had promised to Abraham. Land, seed, blessing.

The promise of seed had certainly been fulfilled. Blessings had come and more blessings were on their way. Now, it was time for land.

And, the people glorified their God

God does hear. He does care about our plight. His timing doesn't always meet our desires but He is always working in our lives.

Look how He spared Moses, how He had Miriam watch by the river, how He planned for Pharaoh's daughter to find him and care about him, how He let his own mother raise him. Moses was always God's plan to rescue His people even when he did not know it.

We are often like Moses arguing with God about our lives and what God wants to do in them. We offer excuses, plead with Him not to send us where we don't want to go. We forget that the great I AM is our God and instead become fearful of those things over which God is in absolute control.

Sometimes we grudgingly obey but when we do obey we can see God's hand move. We become privileged as we see our God actually work through our weaknesses. The outcome is always about Him and His glory – He lets us be a part of His plans.

This day determine not to fear what God has in mind for your life but look for the glory that is to come as you walk in faith with Him.

Chapter Seven

CAMP

The People Complain

1440 - 1400 BC

Moses
Aaron
Joshua
Caleb
Miriam

Exodus 16-40
Leviticus
Numbers
Deuteronomy

The Law
Tabernacle, Feasts and Priesthood
Mutiny and the golden calf
Spying out the land
Rejecting God's Provision
Made to wander in the wilderness

You can take the people out of Egypt but it takes longer to take Egypt out of the people. Even though they had been slaves, they were used to having shelter and food and even a prison gives routine and a semblance of safety.

Now, they were in the wilderness. They lived in tents that they picked up and moved to follow a pillar of fire or cloud. They had no idea where they were heading and this type of living was wearing on them. They began to grumble and complain.

First, it was about water. They came across undrinkable water but the LORD healed the bitter waters and then told them, *"If you will give earnest heed to the voice of the LORD your God, and do what is right in His sight, and give ear to His commandments, and keep all His statutes, I will put none of the diseases on you which I have put on the Egyptians; for I, the LORD, am your healer.*[1]

Then they complained about food and reminisced about their pots of meat back in Egypt. They grumbled against the LORD and against Moses and Aaron. Then the LORD said, *"I will rain bread from heaven for you...and in the morning you will see the glory of the LORD for He hears your grumblings against the LORD; and what are we that you grumble against us?"*[2]

And that evening the Lord brought quails and in the evening the the ground was covered with *"a fine flake-like thing"* that was to be made into bread. They were to gather only what they needed and leave none till the morning just letting the sun melt it. Of course they did not obey until they saw that it turned foul and had worms in it if they kept it.

For 40 years *"what is it"* (manna) fell to the ground 6 days a week. What they saved on the 6th day lasted through the 7th. God was teaching them that He would provide their daily bread. They were to trust Him.

Still they quarreled with Moses about water and asked why he brought them out of Egypt if this would be their life. And the Lord said, *"Behold, I will stand before you there on the rock at Horeb; and you shall strike the rock, and water will come out of it that the people may drink." And Moses did so in the sight of the elders of Israel."*[3]

God provided water yet again. God continues to provide for all of their needs and they continue to doubt.

The Law

Three months after leaving Egypt they come to Mount Sinai. Here the LORD will give the Mosaic Covenant.

This was a provisional covenant that would take the people from this point until the Seed came. Through "the Law" it showed them a way to live before a holy God. It also would show them that it was impossible to keep the Law because of the sin of Adam in them and show them their full need for a Savior.

This law told them that if they obey they would be blessed. If they disobey they would be disciplined. Blessing and curses.

---

1. Exodus 15:26

2. Exodus 16:4

3. Exodus 17:6

Originally the people agree saying that they would do everything the LORD had spoken. Moses goes up to receive the Law on Mount Sinai. The presence of the LORD was like fire upon the mountain and there was thunder and an earthquake and the people get bored while waiting.

Moses had been gone 40 days on the mountain and during that time he was being given information on building the Tabernacle, the Ark of the Covenant, the priestly garments and all instruction of how to live and worship God.

Moses was receiving loving instruction from God for a people He had chosen, grown and set free while they were creating a golden calf to worship.

When the people came complaining to Aaron he didn't call the people back to God but went along with their wishes in order to merge their remembrance of idolatry in Egypt with worship of the Lord who brought them out of it. He helped them to create the golden calf.

We can never water down or compromise the truth and still say we worship God and we cannot expect God to tolerate it.

Aaron who was called to be a leader *"let the people get out of control."* He obeyed the desires of the people rather than the desires of God.

Moses came down from the mountain with the stone tablets written with the finger of God. What he found was a people that had "risen up to play." They were dishonoring themselves and dishonoring God.

Moses called to himself all those who had not worshiped the calf and whose hearts were for the LORD. He instructed them to go among the people and with their sword kill every idolater. Three thousand men fell that day.

The tabernacle is built just as the Lord instructed and the cloud covered the tent by day and fire by night and the glory of the Lord filled the tabernacle. Whenever the cloud lifted they would set out and when it stopped they would set up camp.

You shall be holy for I am holy

God continues in the book of Leviticus to spell out what it is to be holy before Him. From the different offerings to the priestly service to food, childbirth, disease, sex, offenses, festivals, tithes and obedience the people are instructed in the Law.

And God moves the people to the southern edge of the land He has promised them.

The people continue to complain

Land. They were finally at the edge of the land God had promised to Abraham in His covenant with him. Of course, this must be a good time to start grumbling again.

They whined about the fish they remembered eating in Egypt and cucumbers and melons and leeks and onions and garlic but now *"there is nothing at all to look at except this manna."* [4] God is angered with their ungrateful hearts and Moses complains to God about being burdened with such people.

They have rejected the Lord and His provision for them. They saw their enslavement in Egypt as better than freedom with the Lord and His promises. But God says that He will provide meat for them that will last a month until they are sick of it. And He sent quail and more quail and more quail and while they were eating it in their rejection of God and with their ungrateful hearts and their mouths full, many of them died.

Ten against God, Two for God

Moses sends twelve men to spy out the Promised Land. They find it a place *"flowing with milk and honey."* [5] They brought back grapes and figs and pomegranates – some of the produce of the land for all to see. It is indeed a wonderful land that God was giving them.

But....

Ten of the men gave a bad report saying that it *"is a land that devours its inhabitants; and all the people whom we saw in it are men of great size...and we became like grasshoppers in our own sight."* [6]

Only Caleb and Joshua believed God and wanted to go into the land.

> *" "The land which we passed through to spy out is an exceedingly good land. **If the LORD is pleased with us, then He will bring us into this land, and give it to us**-- a land which flows with milk and honey. Only do not rebel against the LORD; and do not fear the people of the land, for they shall be our prey. Their protection has been removed from them, **and the LORD is with us; do not fear them.**"* [7]

---

4. Numbers 11:6

5. Deuteronomy 6:4-9

6. Numbers 13:32

7. Numbers 14:9

Two men believed God to be Who He said that He was. They had seen His miraculous powers move on their behalf. But the people, driven by their fear and lack of faith, picked up stones as if to kill them.

The Lord's judgment

The people had grumbled and tested God ten times. Now they refused to go into the land He was giving them. They would not believe in Him or serve Him.

> And the LORD said to Moses, *"How long will this people spurn Me? And how long will they not believe in Me, despite all the signs which I have performed in their midst?*

> So, the Lord makes a judgement against them. They would not enter the Promised Land. Every adult would die in the wilderness instead of entering the land.

> *Surely all the men who have seen My glory and My signs, which I performed in Egypt and in the wilderness...and have not listened to My voice, shall by no means see the land which I swore to their fathers, nor shall any of those who spurned Me see it...*

> *Your corpses shall fall in this wilderness, even all your numbered men, according to your complete number from twenty years old and upward, who have grumbled against Me...*[8]

Caleb and Joshua, who had stood by the Lord and believed in Him were the only two adults who would step foot in the land. There were over 600,000 men and probably at least as many women who just lost their inheritance in the Abrahamic Covenant.

---

8. Numbers 14:29

> *Surely you shall not come into the land in which I swore to settle you, except Caleb the son of Jephunneh and Joshua the son of Nun. Your children, however, whom you said would become a prey-- I will bring them in, and they shall know the land which you have rejected...*

For every day the land was spied out they would spend one year in the wilderness until that generation had died.

> *And your sons shall be shepherds for forty years in the wilderness, and they shall suffer for your unfaithfulness...according to the number of days which you spied out the land, forty days, for every day you shall bear your guilt a year, even forty years, and you shall know My opposition...* [9]

The final judgment is against those that went with Caleb and Joshua but incited the people against God.

> *As for the men whom Moses sent to spy out the land and who returned and made all the congregation grumble against him by bringing out a bad report concerning the land, even those men who brought out the very bad report of the land died by a plague before the LORD.* [10]

And the people turned back from the edge of the Promised Land to return to the wilderness.

Do we want more than God provides for us? Do we grumble against Him and His provisions? Have we seen the Lord's hand and yet still refuse to believe and obey?

The choice is to be one of the many who reject God or to be the one of the few that believe Him no matter what.

> *"Is the LORD's power limited? Now you shall see whether My word will come true for you or not."* [11]

---

9. Numbers 14:34

10. Numbers 14:37

11. Numbers 11:23

Chapter Eight

CONQUEST

Abrahamic Covenant – Land

1400 - 1020 BC

Joshua
Caleb
Rahab
Deborah & Barak
Gideon
Samson
Samuel
Abimelech
Ruth & Boaz

Joshua
Judges
Ruth
1 Samuel 1-8

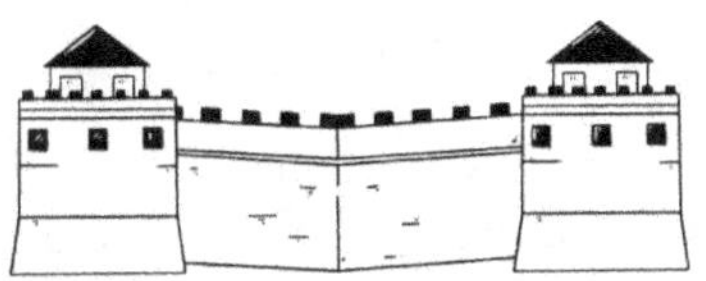

Rahab and the spies
Crossing the Jordan
Capture of Jericho
Battle at Gibeon
Mattle at Merom
Six oppressions of Israel

Forty years have passed and the old generation that came out of Egypt is gone. Now, it is time to finally enter the Promised Land.

The Lord now expands His promise of "land" from the Abrahamic Covenant in the new Palestinian Covenant.

The land they were to be given would be theirs forever. Even if they had been *"outcasts at the ends of the earth, from there the LORD your God will gather you and from there He will bring you back."*[1]

God covenants to bring them into the <u>land</u> in which Abraham had originally lived and to multiply them (<u>seed</u>). God sets before them life and prosperity and death and adversity - their choice. If they love God, walk in His ways, and keep His commandments then they would be <u>blessed</u> in the land. If their hearts turn away and they won't obey and instead worship idols then they shall perish.

> *It is the LORD your God who will cross ahead of you... The LORD your God goes with you... The LORD is the one who goes ahead of you; He will be with you. He will not fail you or forsake you. Do not fear or be dismayed.*[2]

Joshua

Moses has died and leadership now falls to Joshua. The Lord will be with Him as He was with Moses. *"Be strong and very courageous; be careful to do according to all the law...so that you may have success wherever you go."*[3]

Joshua sends two spies into Jericho who are helped by a woman there – Rahab. The inhabitants have heard that the LORD dried up the Red Sea and of their encounters with enemies in their wanderings.

They knew that the LORD had given the Israelites the land and the people feared. But Rahab believed in the LORD and hid the spies. She helped them escape and they promise her refuge. Rahab will join the people of Israel and she will be in the lineage of the Savior.

Crossing the Jordan

When the Hebrews came to the Red Sea when leaving Egypt, Moses raised his hand and the seas parted. This time they need to cross a river in flood stage. The priests are carrying the Ark of the Covenant and the waters do not part until, in faith, they step into the waters.

---

1. Deuteronomy 30:4

2. Deuteronomy 31:8

3. Joshua 1:7

Sometimes we wait for God when we need to move forward in faith. The water coming down the Jordan built up in a heap as the priests stood on dry ground with the ark and the nation crossed the Jordan.

Conquering the Land

The Canaanites, the descendants of Noah's son, Ham, lived in the land and were vile people. They have never repented or turned to the Lord so Joshua is to destroy them completely so that they don't pollute God's people.

God reveals Himself in a new way as *"the captain of the Lord of hosts"*[4] and Joshua fell on his face and worshiped him. The Lord tells him that He has given Jericho to them and tells him how to take the city.

They are to march around the city once a day for six days. Then on the seventh day they are to march around it seven times and then seven priests are to blow their trumpet and everyone should shout and the walls of the city will fall down. And so it did.

Only Rahab and her family were spared and this city of Canaanites was destroyed.

Defeat and Victory

One man, Achan, rather than destroy everything at Jericho took some spoil for himself. This breach of covenant law caused their defeat when they went against the city of Ai. The sin of one man was imputed to the entire nation – they were to be a holy people. Achan's sin had to be cleansed and he died with all that he had. Now they received victory at Ai.

They continued the conquest of southern Canaan and northern Canaan. *"Just as the LORD had commanded Moses his servant, so Moses commanded Joshua, and so Joshua did; he left nothing undone of all that the LORD had commanded Moses."*[5] Complete obedience led to complete victory.

In six years they conquer 31 Kings and take over their territory but they failed to *"utterly destroy"* the ungodly and their influence would bring them great harm in the future.

The land divided

There were twelve tribes from the twelve sons of Israel. Eleven tribes were each given a portion of the land. The tribe of Levi did not receive their own land as this tribe was to

---

4. Joshua 5:14

5. Joshua 11:15

be the priests of God. Their inheritance would be in the Temple serving God rather than a land to own.

And the people settled in to serve the LORD, their God in the land He had given to them.

Seven Cycles of Sin

"The people served the LORD all the days of Joshua." This generation, whose parents had died in the wilderness from lack of faith and disobedience, served the Lord well. Now, a third generation had been born.

> *"There arose another generation after them who did not know the LORD, nor yet the word which He had done for Israel."*[6]

We are always just a generation away from not following God.

These people had not seen the miracles in Egypt or in the desert or been a part of taking the land. They were the descendents of those who did. They did not know the LORD.

> *Then the sons of Israel did evil in the sight of the LORD, and served the Baals, and they forsook the LORD, the God of their fathers, who had brought them out of the land of Egypt, and followed other gods from among the gods of the peoples who were around them, and bowed themselves down to them; thus they provoked the LORD to anger.*[7]

But the ever merciful God raised up Judges to serve them. These people were deliverers and served as military, spiritual and government leaders but the people often rejected or ignored them.

So this sets up the cycle of sin and deliverance.

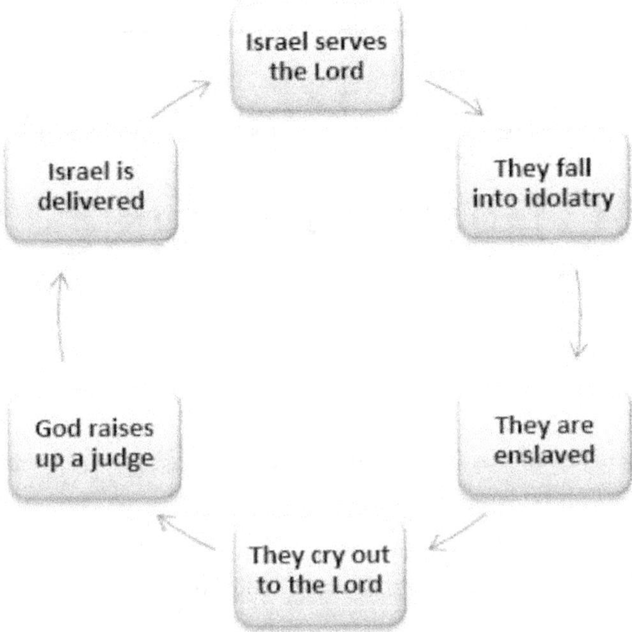

In this time there are the wicked and the wonderful among the people. Gideon, Samson, Deborah, Ruth, and Boaz are all in this time period.

We also see the coming of the prophet, Samuel, sent by the Lord to guide them back to Him. It is a tumultuous time but God reserves for Himself those who will follow Him. He does today as well.

Section 3 – King Saul to Christ the King

From one man in the garden to one man of faith, God has grown Abraham and his family into a nation.

God has been with them directing, loving and protecting these people through the wilderness. He has grown them into a nation and now given them a land of their own.

Unfortunately, they are not consistent in following God even as He is consistent in guiding them. They continue to reject God and in this section they reject Him as Lord over them.

They seek instead to be like the surrounding nations and chose a king for themselves.

This is a section of great tumult and suffering. Their disobedience to the Sovereign Lord and their turning to other "gods" brings curses upon themselves.

The Lord allows them to be overthrown by surrounding nations and taken into captivity. But, as always, He reserves for Himself a remnant that is faithful to Him and He is faithful in restoring them to the land.

And then, The King of Kings comes.

He does not come as a ruler over them but as a servant to them. The seed of the woman foretold in the garden is present to defeat the serpent and to restore all to relationship with God.

And they kill Him.

This King takes on Himself all of the sins of all of mankind realizing the punishment due to make a way back to God. He gives His life allowing His creation to crucify Him in order to pay their penalty.

We end this section holding our breath. Christ returns to heaven, His disciples hide in fear. What has happened?

1 Corinthians 2:8 *none of the rulers of this age has understood; for if they had understood it, they would not have crucified the Lord of glory.*

CROWN

The People Want a King

1020 - 606 BC

Kings
Saul
David
Solomon
Jeroboam
Ahab
Hezekian

Prophets
Samuel
Elijah
Hosea
Isaiah
Jeremiah

Saul chosen
Temple built
Kingdom divided
Golden calves
Elijah challenges Baal
Israel taken captive by Assyria
Reformation under Hezekiah
Judah taken captive by Babylon

1 Samuel 9-31
2 Samuel
1 Kings
2 Kings
1 Chronicles 9-29
2 Chronicles

Poetry
Psalms
Ecclesiastes
Song of Solomon

Prophets
Amos Zephaniah
Hosea Habbakuk
Jonah Obadiah
Joel Jeremiah
Isaiah Nahum

All the others nations have a king and the people of Israel want one too. The elders came to the prophet Samuel and demanded a king to judge them and to go out before them in battles.

And the LORD said to Samuel, "Listen to the voice of the people in regard to all that they say to you, for they have not rejected you, but they have rejected Me from being king over them. Like all the deeds which they have done since the day that I brought them up from Egypt even to this day-- in that they have forsaken Me and served other gods-- so they are doing to you also."[1]

They have moved from reaching out to God to send them a deliverer when they sin and become oppressed to wanting a full time king over them. They have rejected God as their king.

Samuel warned them of what it would be like under a king:

- *he will take your sons and place them for himself in his chariots and among his horsemen and they will run before his chariots.*

- *he will appoint for himself commanders of thousands and of fifties, and some to do his plowing and to reap his harvest and to make his weapons of war and equipment for his chariots.*

- *he will also take your daughters for perfumers and cooks and bakers.*

- *he will take the best of your fields and your vineyards and your olive groves, and give them to his servants.*

- *he will take a tenth of your seed and of your vineyards, and give to his officers and to his servants.*

- *he will also take your male servants and your female servants and your best young men and your donkeys, and use them for his work.*

- he will take a tenth of your flocks, and you yourselves will become his servants.

Then you will cry out in that day because of your king whom you have chosen for yourselves, but the LORD will not answer you in that day.[2]

But they would not listen to reason and so God told Samuel that they could have their desire and the search was made for a king to rule over Israel.

Saul

The first king chosen was Saul. He was the most handsome of men and taller than any of the people. Looking at him from a worldly point of view he was perfect.

This is what they were looking for and God knew it so he had Samuel anoint him as king even though it was a thing which Saul did not want. Saul was anointed and God, ever loving and merciful, sent his Spirit upon Saul to help him.

The problem was that Saul looked good on the outside but on the inside his heart was not truly for God. He did lead the people in battle but he disobeyed the prophet and sinned against the Lord many times and in many ways.

In response, he used excuses, blamed others, tried to justify his actions, and was presumptuous and impatient. Because he had not kept the commandments of the Lord his kingdom would be taken from him.

The LORD wanted *"a man after His own heart"*[3] and it was not Saul. He continued to reject the ways of the Lord and God chose a replacement.

David

The Lord looks at our heart and the heart of David was after his own. He wasn't much in the world's standards. He was merely a boy and a shepherd at that. Samuel anointed David king and *"the Spirit of the Lord came mightily upon David."*[4] The Spirit of the Lord departed from Saul and an evil spirit terrorized him instead.

---

2. 1 Samuel 8:18

3. 1 Samuel 13:14

4. 1 Samuel 16:13

Although David is anointed he does not actually hold the position of king yet. He serves Saul at court, he slays the giant Goliath, he becomes friends with Saul's son, Jonathan and the evil spirit in Saul brought a hatred for David.

David married Saul's daughter but Saul tried to kill him anyway. David had to escape and be on the run. He flees and Saul pursues him all over Israel. David has a band of men who are faithful to the Lord with him and they are on the run together for years until Saul finally dies.

David is crowned as king of Israel and God makes a covenant with him.

Davidic Covenant

Remember the chart on the Abrahamic Covenant? There were three parts to it, National, Personal and Universal. God makes a covenant with David and this covenant comes under the "National" part of the Abrahamic Covenant.

God promises to David a "House," a "Kingdom" and a "Throne" forever. One from David's seed would one day be the king of Israel. You will see how all parts of the Abrahamic Covenant come together in lessons to come. Just remember this part for now.

David, although his heart is for God, is involved in serious sins including adultery and murder. But, he repents and God blesses him with His presence and relationship. Much of the Psalms are a record of David's heart, his struggles, his repentance, and his hope.

Solomon and the Temple

Solomon, a son of David, is the wisest man that has ever lived. He loved the Lord and asks not for wealth or fame but for a heart of understanding to discern between good and evil while he judges over Israel. God is pleased with his request so gives him his wisdom plus wealth and fame.

Solomon's wisdom and heart are recorded in Proverbs, Ecclesiastes and the Song of Solomon.

Solomon built the temple of the Lord and it was magnificent but when he became old his heart was turned away from God by his many wives. He did what was evil and did not follow the Lord.

Civil War and the Kingdom divided

Jeroboam, a servant of Solomon, rebelled against the king. Jeroboam is able to take ten of the tribes to his side and they are then called, "Israel." This civil war left two tribes who were now called, "Judah." The kingdom is divided.

The northern tribes under Jeroboam, for the most part, do not follow the Lord. The tribes under Judah for the most part do.

Israel is taken Captive

Israel has a total of twenty kings and two prophets before the Assyrians take them captive in 722 bc. The Assyrians are a brutal and merciless people and those they take captive they intersperse with their people so that the captives will lose their identity as a people. Thus the ten tribes of Israel are lost.

Judah is taken Captive

Because Judah does follow the Lord some of the time, they are able to stay in the land for a while. God sends them nine prophets to guide and to warn them to follow God but in 586 bc they are taken captive by the Babylonians because their heart for God has turned.

Right now Israel does not have a King on a throne but there is a time coming when Christ will come, the son of David, and sit on the throne to rule on the earth for 1,000 years. The fulfillment of this covenant and the other aspects of the Abrahamic Covenant have been partially fulfilled and yet to be fulfilled.

Chapter Ten

CAPTIVITY 2

No Longer in the Promised Land

Israel 722 BC to...
Juday 606 - 583 BC

<u>Prophets</u>
Jeremiah
Ezekiel
Daniel
Obadiah

<u>Kings</u>
Sargon (Assyria)
Nebuchadnezzar
Belshazzar
Cyrus
Darius

2 Kings 17, 24, 25
2 Chronicles 36:11-23
Ezekiel
Daniel
Jeremiah 40-52
Lamentations
Obadiah

Deportations to Assyria and Babylon
Shadrach, Meshach and Abed-nego
Nebuchadnezzar's dream
The fiery furnace
Daniel and the Ezekiel's visions
Handwriting on the wall
Lion's den

Israel was taken captive by the Assyrians and the Assyrians brought colonists back to the land – this is the beginning of the Samaritan people.

Judah was taken captive by the Babylonians in three stages and by 586 bc the temple is robbed, the city is destroyed and only a few poor remain in the land. But, the ever merciful God promises that after 70 years in captivity He would return them to their land.

They are captives but not slaves in Babylon and are allowed to build houses and make lives for themselves there. They even have some religious freedom. Jeremiah, who had warned them of the coming discipline of the LORD before they were taken, is with them in Babylon. So is Daniel.

Daniel

Nebuchadnezzar, the king, ordered that some of the Hebrew young men who were good-looking, intelligent, wise, discerning and were able to serve him were brought into his court. Among these were Daniel, Hananiah, Mishael and Azariah. These young men were followers of the most high God but had also been taken captive.

Sometimes the godly are impacted by the sins of others.

When they were asked to break God's law regarding eating forbidden food Daniel asked for permission for himself and the others not to defile themselves. God granted Daniel favor with his captors and also gave to them knowledge and wisdom and He gave to Daniel the ability to understand visions and dreams.

The king's dream

No one in Babylon could interpret a disturbing dream of the king – except for Daniel. This dream effects our future.

The dream holds a statue that represents the great kingdoms of the world from the time of Nebuchadnezzar and following. This is a prophetic dream telling of the coming kingdoms of the Medes, Persians, Greeks and Romans – and one kingdom after that which will be set up by *"the God of heaven"* and will never be destroyed. *"It will crush and put an end to all these kingdoms, but it will itself endure forever."*[1]

This final kingdom will be when Christ sits on the throne of David (fulfilling the Davidic and Abrahamic Covenants) and will rule the earth for 1000 years.

The fiery furnace

Daniel's three companions had been renamed. Their original names honored God but their new names, "Shadrach, Meshach and Abed-nego" were given to them to honor the Babylonia gods. Their names were changed but their hearts did not change toward the true God.

When the entire kingdom was ordered to worship an idol or be burned alive these men refused to disobey their God. This civil disobedience is based on their non-negotiable faith in the LORD.

Even when they stand before the fiery furnace they do not try to negotiate with God. Their lives are His and whether they live or die their minds are set on obedience.

---

1. Daniel 2:44

In rage the king throws them into the furnace but when they look into the fire the three young men are walking around and another is with them in the fire. *"The fourth is like a son of the gods!"*[2]

The fire had no effect on them and they didn't even smell of smoke when they came out. The king, humbled by God's display of His power over the king's idol, orders all in the land to honor these men and he sets out to prosper them.

Our hearts, when made up now to serve our God, will be ready for the trials when they come. And our God will deliver us either out of the trial or into His arms.

A life of continual faith

Daniel never wavered from following God in a strange land. All around him was idolatry and worldliness but because He followed God he prospered in the midst of it. Even when his enemies sought to destroy him at 80 years old (they threw him into a lion's den) God continued to uphold Daniel. Daniel is one of the wise men of Babylon.

Toward the end of his life Daniel is given a vision. This vision, like the dream of the king, effects our future. His contemporary, Ezekiel, also has visions of the future for Israel.

70 weeks

Daniel's vision is similar to Nebuchadnezzar's in that it sees four world empires to come. The fourth kingdom in both the dream and the vision represent Rome which will be divided into ten parts. And one will rise after them with the antichrist.

Daniel says that from the time there is a decree to rebuild Jerusalem (still in the future for him) there will be 70 weeks until the end. There is a lot of symbolism in Hebrew writing and 70 weeks here means 70 weeks of years or 490 years.

Just as God had the Hebrews wander one year for every day they spied out the land but wouldn't enter, here we see God holding them responsible for 70 Sabbatical years that they did not keep.

As part of the Law, every seven years they were to let the land rest (Lev 25:1-7) and they had not done this. God would enforce those 70 Sabbaths. Since the Sabbath year only came every 7th year, 70 Sabbaths x 7 years = 490 years.

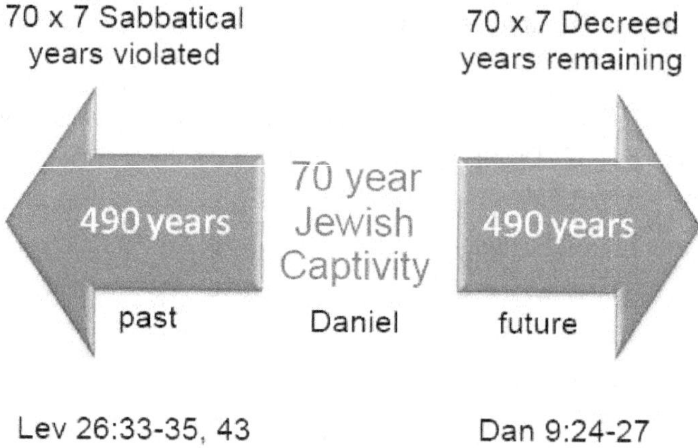

Daniel sees into the future

Daniel says that the Messiah (the one promised way back in the garden) would be cut off after 69 weeks (490 years). Then the last week will come.

The decree to restore Jerusalem does come on March 5, 444 bc, 92 years after Daniel's death. This date starts the beginning of the 70 weeks.

Now if we count forward 69 "weeks" we come to Jesus' triumphal entry into Jerusalem 483 years later where He will be "cut off" or as we know, He will be crucified.

The 70th week, Daniel tells us, will start when a covenant is made with "the Beast." This has not happened yet so we are in the gap between the 69th and 70th week of Daniel's vision closely approaching the tribulation period.

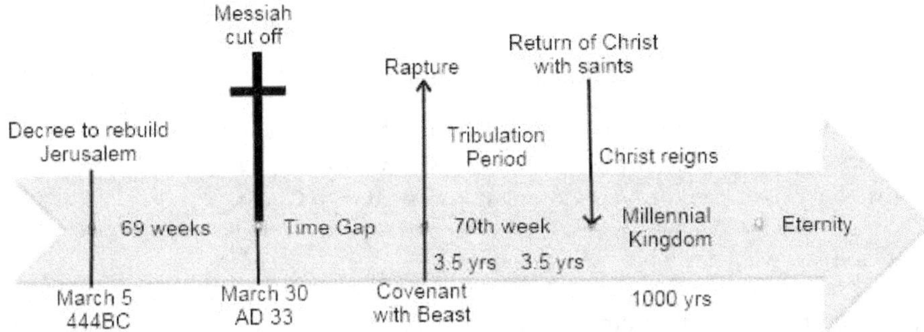

The time gap between the Messiah being cut off and the 70th week is the church age. This is where we are and we are waiting for the last week to begin.

A New Covenant is coming

Jeremiah and Ezekiel had warned the people to repent or that they would fall into captivity. The people did not repent so when Judah was captured, Jeremiah and Ezekiel were taken with the people into Babylon. Before they were called to give warning and now they are there to offer comfort and hope.

The LORD tells both of them of a coming New Covenant. God will, again in His mercy and grace, create a new covenant with them.

> *"I will put My law within them and on their hearts I will write it and I will be their God, and they shall be My people...they shall know Me, from the least of them to the greatest of them...for I will forgive their iniquity, and their sin I will remember no more."*[3]

This is an amazing promise for a people in captivity for abandoning their God.

This new covenant is to be made with the people of Israel so why is it under the "universal" part of the Abrahamic Covenant? Because as we will see in a few more lessons the "Gentiles" (everyone that is not a Jew) will be grafted into this covenant.

---

3. Jeremiah 31:34

Everyone, everywhere can partake of this covenant because of the work of Christ in the new covenant He will institute.

God announces this New Covenant about 500 years before He will bring it to pass.

From our perspective this is good news. Everything that Daniel interpreted in the king's dream has come true. All that he saw in His vision up to the Messiah being cut off has come true. We have seen the New Covenant instituted with Christ.

What God says will be will be.

So, we know that Christ is coming back and that the tribulation is coming. We also know that Christ will sit on the throne of David and that there will be a new heaven and earth and that all God has said will come to pass.

No matter our state or circumstances right now we look to the hope of the promises of our God based on His works in the past and His revelation of Himself to us through His Son and His spirit.

Chapter Eleven

CONSTRUCTION

The End of Captivity

538 - 5 BC

Cyrus
Zerubbabel
Darius
Haggai
Zechariah
Xerxes
Mordecai
Haman
Ezra
Artaxerxes
Nehemiah
Malachi

Ezra
Nehemiah
Esther
Haggai
Zechariah
Malachi

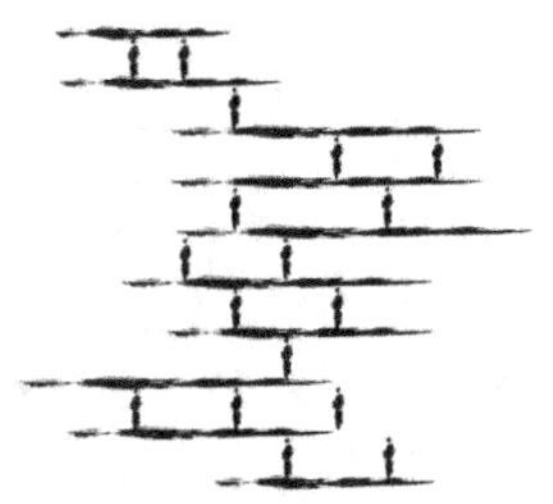

Return under Zerubbabel - Temple rebuilt
Return under Ezra - Reformation
Return of Nehemiah - Wall rebuilt
Close of the Old Testament - 400 years of silence

Babylon had been conquered by the Persians, the next great empire, as was foretold in Nebuchadnezzar's dream.

What God says will come to pass does and the LORD had said that their captivity would be 70 years. That time had come.

God works in the heart of Cyrus, the Persian king, and he is moved to issue a proclamation in 538 bc that all those who wish to may return to the land.

Of the captives from the two tribes of Judah, 42,500 say that they will return to the land. They are led by Zerubbabel and they build an altar for worship. They begin the foundation of the temple which is partially financed by their former captors.

The enemies of Judah approach them to discourage and frighten. They even hire public relations experts to frustrate their efforts with Cyrus and Darius, the king that followed Cyrus. They are opposed and forced to stop the work.

But, God sends Haggai and Zechariah to encourage the people to continue the work and in four years the temple is finished. This is the second temple. It is 516 bc.

The second return

Eighty years after the first return to the land a second contingent will return. It is now 458 bc. Artaxerxes is king and he allows all that wish to return to the land. God even has the king finance the journey and they are given the right to have civil rulers over them although they will still be under the domain of Persia.

This group of about 2000 is led by Ezra. What he finds is not a people restored to following God but a people who:

- neglect the Law

- intermarry with the inhabitants of the land

Ezra exhorts them to turn back to the Lord and His ways and they leave their heathen wives. He leads the people back to worship the Lord their God.

The third return

Although some people have returned to the land, some are still in Persia. Nehemiah, a high officer in the Persian court, is grieved about the state of Jerusalem. The report he receives is that the people are in great distress and reproach, the walls are broken down and the gates are burned.

Nehemiah immediately goes to prayer.

For days he weeps and mourns and he fasts and prays before God. He confesses the sins of the people of Israel and asks God to remember his covenant and his promise to Moses:

> *"Remember the word which Thou didst command Thy servant Moses, saying, 'If you are unfaithful I will scatter you among the peoples; but if you return to Me and keep My commandments and do them, though those of*

you who have been scattered were in the most remote part of the heavens, I will gather them from there and will bring them to the place where I have chosen to cause My name to dwell.[1]

The king notices Nehemiah's demeanor and when he finds out the cause of his sadness he asks Nehemiah what he wanted. Again, Nehemiah says a quick prayer and then he asks for permission to leave to rebuild the city.

On March 5, 444 bc a decree is issued to rebuild and restore Jerusalem. **This decree starts the beginning of Daniel's 70 weeks.**

Nehemiah returns and organizes the people to work and stand watch against their enemies. The walls to the city are rebuilt in just fifty-two days. He then rules as governor.

So, the people are back to the land, the walls and temple are rebuilt and dedicated and the Law is read. The people repent and renew their commitment to keep God's laws.

Malachi

About 100 years have passed since the return to the land. Although there was revival under Nehemiah that enthusiasm has worn off. They move to religion and are lax in keeping the tithe but can't fathom why God is not pleased with them.

God raises up Malachi to rebuke the people for moving to religion instead of true worship and calls them to repentance.

"I, the LORD, do not change; therefore you, O sons of Jacob, are not consumed."[2] God does not change so He remains faithful to His covenant even when the people are not. He calls them back to Himself and the Old Testament closes.

400 years of silence

No new prophet is sent to Israel for 400 years. God appears silent. But much happens in the world.

As prophesied, the Babylonian empire gives way to the Persian Empire who gives way to Alexander the Great and the Grecian empire who gives way to the empire of Rome.

God may be silent but He is preparing for the coming of the promised seed.

---

1. Nehemiah 1:8-9

2. Malachi 3:6

With the institution of the Roman Empire a common language is instituted. The Roman roads reach into the whole empire and the "Pax Romana" ensures safety for travelers. Hence, when Christ arrives the word will be able to travel to the known world quickly and easily.

Daniel has taught the wise men of the coming of the Messiah and that knowledge has been passed down. The wise men that will "see His star" and travel from the east to find Him have this knowledge because of Daniel.

The Jews have divided themselves into religious groups: the Pharisees, Sadducees, the Essenes, the Scribes and Herodians.

Into this world the Immanuel will come.

God does not give up on His covenants and promises and we should not give up waiting for their fulfillment.

Like Ezra, we can call one another back to worship and holiness. Like Nehemiah, our hearts can grieve over the brokenness we see and we can pray for God's hand and for what we can do for His people.

And, even if we do not see God moving we can know that He is always working out His purposes even through ungodly people and nations.

Chapter Twelve

CHRIST

The Promised One

3 BC - 33 AD

Jesus
Mary
Joseph
Angel Gabriel
John the Baptist
Satan
Nicodemus
Mary, Marth, Lazarus
Mary Magdalene
Peter, James, John
Andrew, Matthew
Herod the Great
Pilate
Herod Antipas

Matthew
Mark
Luke
John
Acts 1

Bethlehem
Flight to Egypt
Childhood in Nazareth
Baptism
Tempted in the desert
12 apostles
Sermon on the Mount

Transfiguration
Raising of Lazarus
Triumphal entry
Olivet Discourse
Betrayal of Judas
Arrest and trial
Crucifixion
Resurrection
Ascension

In Genesis He was the promised seed of the woman who would crush the head of the serpent. In the Abrahamic Covenant He was the way to blessing for all nations. In the Davidic Covenant He was the one who would sit on the throne and rule forever.

In every book of Scripture we can see the foretelling and forthcoming Savior. For generations the world has waited. People have been born, lived and died for centuries without seeing the Messiah. And then, in the fullness of time, He comes.

Immanuel

He comes to a virgin, He comes as a baby. The all-powerful God humbles Himself and takes on human flesh. He is "God with us."

The world has been waiting – creation itself has been waiting for the revealing of the Savior and His restoration.

For Jesus' first 30 years of life not much is written about Him. He does not reveal Himself until He comes to be baptized by John the Baptist.

John recognized Him and didn't want to baptize Him but the Lord insisted in order to do two things,

1) to identify with the sinners He had come to save, and

2) to fulfill all requirements for Him to be Israel's Messiah.

Part of that requirement was that He would be of the line of David.

Davidic Lineage

God had promised that the Savior would sit on the throne of David. This means that He would have to be a direct descendant of him.

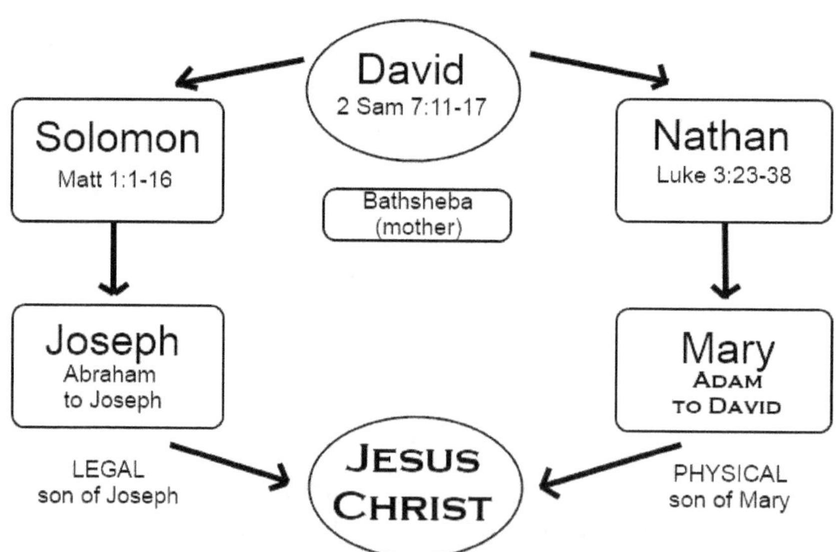

Matthew relates Jesus' genealogy to prove that He has the right to be the king of the Jews. He is a legal descendant of Joseph for even though He is not of Joseph's blood line He is a part of his family and therefore a legal heir. He was born of Mary so He has the physical heritage to be king of the Jews.

Why four Gospels?

There is a reason the Lord told of His Son in four accounts. Each Gospel speaks to different people with a different aspect of the Savior.

- **Matthew** is writing to the Jews and shows Christ as the promised <u>Messiah and King</u> – the son of David fulfilling the promises of the Old Testament.

- **Mark** is writing to the Gentiles. He doesn't include the things that a Jewish audience would seek but instead presents Christ as the <u>suffering Servant</u> who came to serve and give His life a ransom for many.

- **Luke**, the only Gentile writer, is a physician and historian seeking to write an orderly, historical account based on the reports of eye witnesses. His purpose is to show that faith in the <u>Son of Man</u> is based on actual and verifiable events.

- **John's** Gospel is different than the other three in that it contains theological writing in regards to Jesus and faith. He shows Jesus to be the <u>Son of God</u>. He speaks of the deity of Jesus as the *"Word"* and that the *"Word was God."* He writes of the events and miracles of Jesus so *"that you may believe that Jesus is the Christ, the Son of God, and that by believing you may have life in his name."*[1]

Temptation of the Christ

After His baptism, the Spirit of God descends upon Him and His Father says, *"This is My beloved Son, in whom I am well-pleased."*[2]

He is led by the Spirit into the wilderness to fast and pray. This is a place to focus, of solitude, of prayer and meditation. It is a place of strength. But His physical body is weakened from the fast and the evil one attempts to take advantage of this.

He tempts Jesus in the same three ways he tempted Eve and he tempts us today:

- Stop fasting and eat – <u>lust of the flesh</u> – be independent from God's will.

- Show yourself, you don't need to be humble – <u>pride of life</u>- be self-sufficient.

- Worship me and rule the world – <u>lust of the eyes</u> – power and authority.

---

1. John 20:31

2. Matthew 3:17, Matthew 17:5, Mark 1:11, Mark 9:7, Luke 3:22, Luke 9:35, 2 Peter 1:17

Jesus uses the Word of God to combat the evil one. Here and throughout His life He was tempted in all ways just as we are but He never sinned. He understands what our lives are like for He has walked in our shoes.

His Ministry

Jesus begins His ministry by quoting a prophecy about Himself from Isaiah 61:1-2.

> *"The Spirit of the Lord is upon Me, because He anointed Me to <u>preach the gospel</u> to the poor. He has sent Me to proclaim <u>release to the captives,</u> and recovery of <u>sight to the blind,</u> to <u>set free</u> those who are downtrodden, to <u>proclaim</u> the favorable year of the Lord."* [3]

(He stopped in the middle of verse 2. We exist in between the first and second part of the verse. The second part is *"and the day of vengeance of our God."* The coming of Christ starts the verse with good news, healing, freedom, and sight to those blinded by the evil one. We await the time when God will bring judgment on the world, the evil one will be defeated and all will be restored.)

> *And He closed the book, and gave it back to the attendant, and sat down; and the eyes of all in the synagogue were fixed upon Him. And He began to say to them, "Today this Scripture has been fulfilled in your hearing."*

No one had ever spoken like that in the synagogue for there had never been one who could fulfill it. But they were enraged that the son of Joseph, as they thought Him to be, would make such a claim. So, they tried to drive Him out but He walked right through their midst.

He gathered 12 disciples and began to instruct them. As they traveled about He healed, forgave sin, performed miracles, rebuked the religious, raised the dead and loved all.

He spoke of the coming Kingdom of God and invited all who would come to come. He taught in parables and fulfilled all of the over 400 prophecies that had been foretold about Him.

At times great crowds would follow Him. Some came to see Him perform a miracle others out of curiosity and still others for they longed for salvation and they hoped Him to be the Messiah.

---

3. Luke 4:18-19

Eight Sign-Miracles

We have some recorded miracles and we are told that He performed more than could be written in all the books on earth. Here are the recorded ones from the book of John:

1. He turned water into wine[4]

2. He healed the royal official's son[5]

3. He healed the invalid at Bethesda[6]

4. He feed the 5,000[7]

5. He walked on the water[8]

6. He brought sight to the blind[9]

7. He raised Lazarus from the dead[10]

8. He gave a miraculous catch of fish[11]

He showed Himself to be Lord over creation, over life and over death. The religious leaders of the day hated Him for it.

How dare He come and proclaim freedom to the captives. They followed the Law, after all, and He seemed to think He was above it. Add to this that He actually claimed to be the great "I AM." They plotted to kill Him.

The I AM:

- I am the bread of life[12]

---

4. John 2:1-11

5. John 4:46-54

6. John 5:1-9

7. John 6:1-14

8. John 6:15-21

9. John 9:1-41

10. John 11:1-44

11. John 21:1-14

12. John 6:35

- I am the light of the world[13]

- I am the gate[14]

- I am the good shepherd[15]

- I am the resurrection and the life[16]

- I am the way, the truth and the life[17]

- I am the true vine[18]

- Before Abraham was born, I AM[19]

Jesus claimed to be God and proved it by His names, His attributes, His works and His acceptance of worship. He exposed darkness and the darkness hated Him and had to extinguish His light.

Israel throughout her years was sent prophets to help them. They didn't listen; they openly mocked them, blamed them for their problems, stoned them and now they would kill the Son of God sent to save them.

What happened on the cross?

Jesus came to die on the cross. Before He created the universe He knew He would come to die for us. He knew Adam would sin and that all that were in Him would be born in sin. He knew that sinful people could not live a holy life before a holy God.

If people were to be saved He would have to do it Himself.

He had made a covenant with Eve to send a Messiah. He had made a further covenant with Abraham to bless all nations through His seed and He had made a further covenant with David that his seed would sit on the throne forever.

God keeps His covenants.

---

13. John 8:12

15. John 10:11, 14

16. John 11:25

17. John 11:25

18. John 15:1,5

19. John 8:58

At the cross, the One who had lived a sinless life, as Adam and all in him had not, took on all of the sins of all of humanity. Sin had declared us guilty of high treason against the Holy One. Death was the punishment. And here was Christ stepping in to take that punishment.

A just and righteous God could not overlook sin or He would not be just and righteous.

Treason required punishment and Christ took that punishment for us. He is the payment due. As a matter of fact from the cross He says, "*It is finished.*"[20] It means, "paid in full" and was the term written in that time on a debt note when it is paid.

You and I were in Christ at the cross just as we had been in Adam at birth.

What happened at the resurrection?

Christ has been raised from the dead, the first fruits of those who are asleep. For since by a man came death, by a man also came the resurrection of the dead. For **as in Adam all die, so also in Christ all shall be made alive.**

"The first man, Adam, became a living soul. The last Adam (Jesus) *became a life-giving spirit.*

But now Christ has been raised from the dead, the first fruits of those who are asleep.

For since **by a man came death, by a man also came the resurrection of the dead.** *For as in Adam all die, so also in Christ all shall be made alive.*"[21]

---

20. John 19:30

21. 1 Corinthians 15

Christ's death in your place and mine brought forgiveness of our sins and gave us eternal life. Here's why.

We changed identity. Our standing with God comes from our birth. If we are still in Adam then we are still dead in our sins. But, when we are in Christ we are raised to newness of life and are identified with Him forever.

God now looks at us "in Christ." And we will be considered this way forever. Think of it this way, Christ was treated as if He had lived like us and now we will be treated as if we lived like Him.

The promised New Covenant came in Jesus Christ. The new heart and new spirit that Jeremiah and Ezekiel had foretold were now available to all who would believe.

Some say that Jesus wasn't resurrected but He appeared to Mary Magdalene, Peter, two disciples on the road to Emmaus, ten disciples in the upper room, eleven disciples a week later, to seven disciples at the Sea of Galilee, over 500 believers, to James, to the eleven again and one last time at His resurrection.

He ate, He travelled, He spoke, He was touched and seen as the resurrected Christ.

Christ returns to the Father.

His work done, Christ returns to be with the Father in heaven. He leaves a command: *"Make disciples – baptizing and teaching them in the name of the Father, and the Son and the Holy Spirit."* [22] Just as His ministry on earth began with all three person of the Trinity it will end the same way.

And He gives a promise: *"I am with you always, even to the end of the age."* [23]

The disciples had been frightened after the crucifixion. They had hidden themselves venturing out only to see the empty tomb and then Christ had come to them. Now, they had watched Him return to heaven.

He had told them to wait to receive power from the Holy Spirit so they waited.

---

22. Matthew 29:18

23. Matthew 29:20

Section 4 – The Church on Earth to the Heavenly Kingdom

There had been families, peoples and nations, kings and paupers, the wise and the foolish, palaces and temples but never had there been the church.

Where, in the past, God's Spirit came upon some individuals to guide and help, now He would take up residence inside those that were His. They would be the temple of the Lord and a nation of priests to Him.

> *"I will put My law within them, and on their heart I will write it; and I will be their God, and they shall be My people."* [1]

The New Covenant promised by God to Jeremiah was sealed in the blood of Christ.

*"This cup which is poured out for you is the **new covenant** in My blood."* [2]

The power of sin is broken and all that is left is for all peoples everywhere to hear of the good news and then the presence of sin to be destroyed forever.

Had the evil one known that now Christ would be present in power in everyone who is born again he never would have crucified Him. Now, those who in faith put their trust in Christ are new creations with Christ alive in them.

---

1. Jeremiah 31:33

2. Luke 22:20

> *Of this church I was made a minister according to the stewardship from God bestowed on me for your benefit, that I might fully carry out the preaching of the word of God that is, the mystery which has been hidden from the past ages and generations; but has now been manifested to His saints, to whom God willed to make known what is the riches of the glory of this mystery among the Gentiles, which is* **Christ in you, the hope of glory.** [3]

The story of God's redemption that started in the garden is about to be completed. His grace, mercy, lovingkindness and faithfulness are evident and His people will glorify Him forever and ever.

---

3. Colossians 1:25-27

Chapter Thirteen

CHURCH

The Holy Spirit Comes

30 AD until Christ returns

Peter
Stephen
Philip
Paul
Priscilla
Barnabas
Silas
James
Mark
Junia
Timothy
Titus
Luke

Acts to Revelation 3

Church is born at Pentecost
Witness in Jerusalem
Witness in Judea
Witness in Samaria
Witness in all the world
Church becomes religion - Dark Ages
Reformation - missions revitalized
Becoming like the world
Waiting for Christ to return

The church starts when the Holy Spirit comes. For ten days since the Lord returned to heaven, the apostles and disciples have been waiting. They choose a replacement for Judas and continually devote themselves to being together and to prayer.

And then He comes.

A violent rushing wind is heard and tongues of fire land upon those of faith. The Holy Spirit takes up residence within them.

They begin to speak with languages they do not know. People from all nations were in Jerusalem and they rush to see what has happened. They hear the Spirit filled disciples, men and women, speak in their own language the *"mighty deeds of God."*[1]

Peter suddenly is enabled to stand and give a great sermon. He proclaims the good news of the resurrection and ascension of Jesus Christ to which they were witnesses. The speech is God-inspired and God-empowered and the people are pierced to the heart.

Peter tells them to repent, be baptized in the name of Jesus Christ for the forgiveness of their sins and that they too would receive the Holy Spirit. Three thousand people do that day.

People had *"a sense of awe; and many wonders and signs were taking place through the apostles."*[2] The church starts with power!

The New Covenant

"This cup which is poured out for you is the new covenant in My blood." Jeremiah had talked of a new covenant to come and Christ initiated it with His own blood.

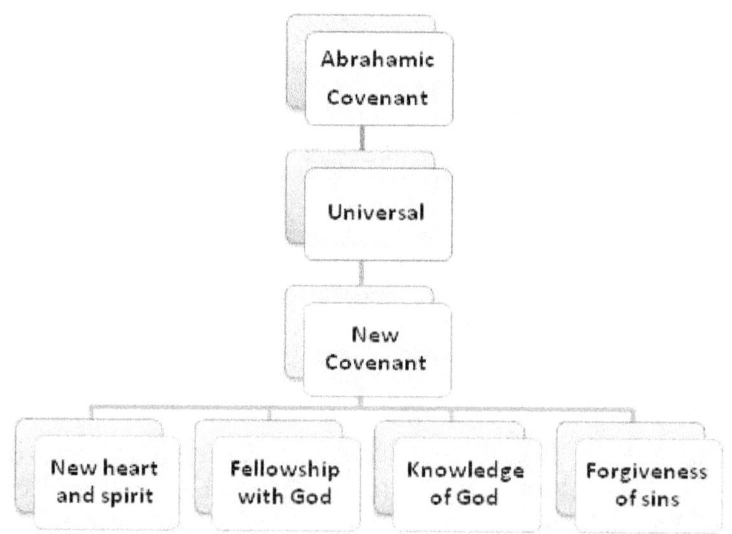

They had been given a new heart and spirit, they now had fellowship with God for the Spirit of Christ lived within them, they had a new understanding of God and His

---

1. Acts 2:11

2. Acts 2:43

promises and they had received forgiveness for their sins. *"Then they will be My people, and I shall be their God."* [3]

The New Church at Jerusalem

The believers were together. They were the first people to be called "the church." And because they were a new people they saw everything they had as belonging to all. Those that had surplus sold it to share with those of the church that had need.

They were devoting themselves to the apostles teaching and to fellowship together and to breaking bread and to prayer. With one mind they went to the temple and house to house together taking meals with gladness and sincerity of heart, praising God.

And the Lord added to their numbers daily.

At Judea and Samaria

Before leaving Christ had told them to be witnesses first in Jerusalem then in all Judea and Samaria and then to the most remote part of the earth. The church was growing in Jerusalem and it needed to start moving outward.

Persecution started that movement. As Christ-followers began feeling oppressed they moved outward from Jerusalem and brought with them the good news of salvation through Jesus Christ.

And those that scattered preached the Word. And the church grew!

Saul

Saul, a zealous Jew, saw it as his duty to stop this blasphemous sect called, "Christians." He pursued them and stood in approval as Stephen was martyred.

And then he met Jesus.

On the road to Damascus he and his companions were suddenly surrounded by light and he heard a voice asking, *"Saul, Saul, why are you persecuting Me?"* [4] The voice told Him that He was Jesus and that Saul was to go into the city and he would be told what to do.

His companions were speechless and Saul was left blinded. They took him to Damascus where the Lord had waiting a man named, "Ananias."

---

3. Ezekiel 11:20

4. Acts 9:4

Ananias went to Saul and told him that Jesus had sent him that he might regain his sight and be filled with the Spirit. Immediately he received his sight and was baptized and began to proclaim Jesus.

Three years later Saul, now called "Paul," heads out to spread the word. Why three years? The Lord took him to Arabia where he was alone with God and being prepared for his ministry to come. He needed time to learn and unlearn, to be equipped and humbled.

To the Uttermost Parts of the Earth

Christ had appointed Paul as a missionary to the Gentiles. Jesus came first to the Jews, God's chosen people, but the blessing was to be universal. All nations would be blessed through the coming of the Lord (Abrahamic Covenant).

Although some Gentiles had come to a saving knowledge of Jesus Christ it was only a handful compared to the rest of the known world. Paul sets out on three separate missionary journeys starting churches as he goes and writing letters that later become included in Scripture.

Many Jews rejected Jesus as their Messiah as they had rejected God so many times before. He had come to them and they did not recognize Him.

So, God *"grafted in"* the Gentiles into the promise and people of many languages, cultures, nations and people groups now recognize Christ as their God and King.

*And coming to Him as to a living stone, rejected by men, but choice and precious in the sight of God, you also, as **living stones**, are being built up as **a spiritual house** for **a holy priesthood**, to offer up spiritual sacrifices acceptable to God through Jesus Christ. For this is contained in Scripture: "Behold I lay in Zion a choice stone, a precious corner stone, and he who believes in Him shall not be disappointed."*

*But you are **a chosen race, a royal priesthood, a holy nation, a people for God's own possession**, that you may proclaim the excellencies of Him who has called you out of darkness into His marvelous light; for you once were not a people, but now you are the people of God; you had not received mercy, but now you have received mercy.*[5]

---

5. 1 Peter 2:5

The Church since

The church was persecuted for two hundred years but then became the state church around the year 400 ad.

The church moved from the simplicity of worshipping the Lord into an organized religion even barring Christians from owning or reading Scripture in order to maintain power and control. Many were burned at the stake for having a Bible.

Corruption grew and the church barely resembled the first days when the Holy Spirit came.

The "church" holds the people captive with fear of hell unless they do what the church wants. It becomes the giver of salvation and starts its own "law" that no one can keep. The freedom the Lord had taught and brought barely exists.

Around 1500 ad reformation came through Martin Luther who pointed out the corruption in the institutionalized church and wanted everyone to be able to read and know Scripture.

Around 1800 interest in missions renewed and people were sent to the farthest reaches of the earth to once again proclaim Christ.

Today much of the world has lost its Christian foundation. Apostasy abounds. The pureness of the Word is diluted with false religions, humanism, idolatry, paganism, political correctness and conforming to the world.

The excitement of the first church and the love it had amongst the members and for Christ and His world seems to have waned. But, God always reserves a remnant for Himself.

And we wait for Christ to return.

Chapter Fourteen

CHRIST RETURNS

Christ Meets the Church in the Air

Any Day

Christ the King
Church
Antichrist
False Prophet
Satan
144,000 Witnesses
Two witnesses
Harlot
Israel
Gentiles

Rapture and Bema Seat
Antichrist
Judgments
Satan cast to earth
Return of Christ in glory
Armageddon
Beast and false prophet into lake of fire
Satan bound for 1000 years
Judgment of the nations

1 Corinthians 15
1 Thessalonians 4, 5
Matthew 24, 25
Luke 21
Mark 13
Revelation

Generations are born, live and die waiting for Christ to return as He said that He would and they pass to their offspring the promise and hope of His coming. We too watch the skies and listen for the trumpet that will signal His return for us - the church.

Jesus said that He would return at a time that we do not expect Him so we are to be watching, longing for our Lord to come to us. But, He will not come yet to the Earth, we will meet Him in the air. This is what is called "the rapture."[1]

---

1. In seminary we learned how to debate for and against the different eschatological beliefs.

> 1 Thess. 4:17 *For the Lord Himself will descend from heaven with a shout, with the voice of the archangel, and with the trumpet of God; and the dead in Christ shall rise first. Then we who are alive and remain shall be caught up together with them in the clouds to meet the Lord in the air, and thus we shall always be with the Lord.* [2]

We will be instantly changed from our corruptible bodies to incorruptible, from mortal to immortal (1 John 3:2) and we will be with Him forever.

Rewards

Every believer will stand before the "Bema seat" of Christ. In Roman and Greek culture this was a place to receive rewards for accomplishments similar to the Olympics.

Christ tells us that we will stand before Him as well. Our lives will be examined, not for judgment or salvation, for salvation is a gift and not earned, but to be rewarded for serving Him with our hearts and lives.

Some people will find that as Christ tests their works much of it survives the test. They have lived for Him and receive rewards from Him for being a good and faithful servant. The joy of His pleasure at our lives lived from our love for Him must be greater, sweeter and more wonderful than can be imagined.

Some people will find themselves weeping as their tested works show that they lived not for Christ but for themselves. What they benefited on Earth will be their only reward for eternity. They have made it to heaven as one escaping a fire with only the clothes on their backs (1 Cor 3:15).

To see the Lord who died for us face to face without sin and to realize that this magnificent, glorious, loving God is the One they could have served and did not will be devastating.

While we stand before the Lord much is going on in the Earth we left behind.

Great tribulation on the Earth

After Christians are taken to Heaven all hell breaks loose on Earth.

---

2. 1 Thessalonians 4:16-17

Israel makes a covenant with the antiChrist who is empowered by satan. He sets himself up as god and can actually do signs and wonders that deceive the world as to his true nature.

The world falls in love with him and receives his mark. They willingly receive it for without it one would be unable to participate in society and unable even to buy food. The nations of the world also pledge him their allegiance and worship him.

In the second half of this seven year period the antiChrist breaks the covenant he made previously with Israel and the "great tribulation" begins.

The beast kills the two witnesses God sends to the Earth. God seals 144,000 witnesses from the twelve tribes of Israel as the antiChrist turns savagely on Israel.

God casts satan and his angels to the Earth and away from His presence.

The book of Revelation speaks of three sets of judgments during this time. These judgments show themselves as great wars and famines, disease and natural disasters that will wipe billions off the face of the Earth.

> *Then there will be a great tribulation, such as has not occurred since the beginning of the world until now, nor ever shall* [3]

The Beast, otherwise known as the antiChrist joins the leaders of the world together to fight against the Lord. They gather together at Armageddon to wait for Him.

The Seven Seals 6:1-8:6

- Antichrist
- War
- Famine
- Death
- Martyrs protest
- Great Earthquakes
- Announcement of the Seven Trumpet Judgments

The Seven Trumpets 8:7-9:21

- A third of the vegetation is burned up
- A third of the sea is judged
- A third of the fresh water is judged
- A third of the stars darkened
- Increased demonic activity
- A third of all people killed
- Announcement of the seven bowl judgments

The Seven Bowls 15:1-16:21

- Malignant sores
- The sea turns to blood
- Fresh water turns to blood
- People are scorched with fire
- Darkness comes over the kingdom of the beast
- Invasion from the east
- Greatest earthquake and widespread destruction

Coming to Establish His Kingdom

And Jesus comes.

This time He returns with all of the saints and the armies of heaven. But there is no clash of weapons, there is no real fight because satan, the antiChrist, the demons and the people of the Earth stand before the Almighty God. They have no real power. There is no actual contest.

The antiChrist and his false prophet are seized and thrown into the lake of fire. With His word the Lord destroys all those assembled against Him. And satan is thrown into the abyss to be imprisoned for 1000 years.

The judgment of the Gentiles

Christ judges all non-Israelites that survived the great tribulation (Mat 25:31-46). How they treated His people, Israel, during this time has shown their heart toward God. Those who have been kind to the people risked much during the time of the antiChrist and they are allowed to come into the Kingdom. Those who did nothing or joined in persecution are sent to everlasting fire.

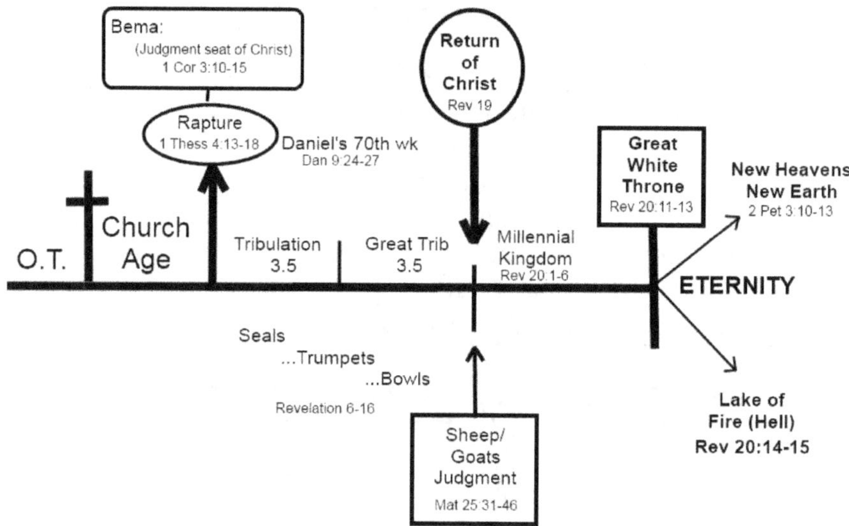

Chapter Fifteen

CHRIST THE KING

On the Throne of David

1000 year reign on Earth

Christ
Satan
God, the Father
Gentiles
Israel
Wicked Dead

Revelation 20
Isaiah 11
Psalm 2
Ezekiel 40-48

Return of the King of all Kings
Resurrection of the rest of the saved
Israel regathers
Land given to Israel
Rebuilding the Temple
Satan revolts
Destruction of rebellion by fire
Judgment
Wicked into the lake of fire

Remember the Abrahamic Covenant? God promised Abraham that He would make Abraham great, that a nation would come from him and that all nations of the Earth would be blessed through His descendant.

God fulfills His promise to Abraham in Christ. All nations are blessed because of Him. Christ reigns now as their King.

Remember the Palestinian Covenant? In it, God reconfirmed His promise that the people of Israel would have a land of their own. Israel is now regathered to the promised land.

Remember the Davidic Covenant? God promised David that his descendent would sit on the throne. We have seen that Jesus is the legal descendent of David. Now THE King is present and ruling the Earth.

Satan has been bound for a thousand years and Christ is reigning as God had promised. He rules in truth and righteousness and there is peace over the entire world.

With Christ on the throne all the covenants the Lord had made have been fulfilled.

What is the kingdom like?

After the tribulation there had been great changes to the Earth. There had been much devastation but God also brought great good. God told Isaiah of these days so he could tell us what life would be like in the Millennial Kingdom.

> *And the wolf will dwell with the lamb, and the leopard will lie down with the kid, and the calf and the young lion and the fatling together; and a little boy will lead them. Also the cow and the bear will graze; their young will lie down together; and the lion will eat straw like the ox. And the nursing child will play by the hole of the cobra, and the weaned child will put his hand on the viper's den. They will not hurt or destroy in all My holy mountain, for the earth will be full of the knowledge of the LORD As the waters cover the sea.*

> *And the light of the moon will be as the light of the sun, and the light of the sun will be seven times brighter, like the light of seven days, on the day the LORD binds up the fracture of His people and heals the bruise He has inflicted.* [1]

There is no crime with the King present. All live in peace and even the earth and heavens appear to have been partially restored. Anyone living at this time would be able to enjoy a lifestyle almost like the garden God created in the beginning.

Finally there is peace and there is rest.

Satan-led revolt

---

1. Isaiah 11:6-9, 30:26

All is not finished though. When the thousand years are completed satan is released. He again goes out to deceive the nations and to gather them to fight the Lord. Sadly, after so long with the presence of God, with peace in all ways, with truth and righteousness and the love of God the nations turn from the Lord to again follow satan.

The King has ruled them well but they have not come to love Him nor do they want Him to reign over them. They will not submit.

The nations come to Jerusalem and surround it to destroy it but God sends down fire from Heaven and destroys them all instead. Again, there is no real battle and they are deceived to think that there could be.

God then causes satan to join the beast and false prophet in the lake of fire. No longer will he be a presence to deceive the nations into high treason. He will be tormented there forever.

Wicked before the Great White Throne

If you were to find yourself at the Great White Throne for judgment you would be in great trouble. This judgment, unlike the Bema seat, is not a place of reward but a place for punishment.

The wicked of all time are brought before God. Their works are revealed before Him so that they cannot contest His judgment. It will be proved that they are wicked, that they did not want Christ and that they deserve punishment.

Those who have lived a "good" life will be unable to defend themselves for the standard for goodness is Christ and all "good" that we do apart from Him is worthless. It is faith in Christ and His works that justifies us and we cannot be justified by anything apart from Him.

All the wicked are sent to join satan in the lake of fire. They did not want God and that is what they shall have for eternity.

Chapter Sixteen

COMPLETION

New Heavens and Earth

Eternity

God, the Father
God, the Son
God, the Holy Spirit
Bride of Christ

Isaiah 66:22
1 Corinthians 15:24-28
2 Peter 3
Revelation 21-22

New heavens and new Earth
New Jerusalem
God and people face to face
Perfect holiness
God's plan of salvation completed

The old Earth and the old heavens have also been restored. No longer does creation groan to be redeemed for God has cleansed it of all sin and evil. A new city has been readied to come down from heaven to the new earth.

New Jerusalem

Think of a cube – an amazingly large cube. It is 1500 miles wide and long and tall. That would cover ½ of the United States in width and then go 1500 miles straight up. That is the New Jerusalem! But there is more.

There are twelve foundations made of precious stones, twelve gates each made from a single, giant pearl with the name of one of the tribes of Israel. The streets of the city are paved with gold so pure it is like transparent glass. The city shines with the glory of God.

And the city has no need of the sun or of the moon to shine on it, for the glory of God has illumined it, and its lamp is the Lamb.[1]

There is no temple *for the Lord God the Almighty and the Lamb are its temple.* The gates are never closed and the people bring into the city the honor of the nations and the glory of kings. There is no evil or anything unclean in this city for *only those whose names are written in the Lamb's book of life* are here.

Perfect Age

From the throne of God a river emanates. It is the river of life and on either side of this river is the tree of life, bearing twelve kinds of fruit, yielding its fruit every month; and the leaves of the tree were for the healing of the nations.

There will no longer be any curse; and the throne of God and of the Lamb will be in it, and His bond-servants will serve Him; they will see His face, and His name will be on their foreheads.

And He shall wipe away every tear from their eyes; and there shall no longer be any death; there shall no longer be any mourning, or crying, or pain; the first things have passed away.[2]

God and man are together with no curse, no sin, nothing in the way. Perfection.

God is All in All – Eternity.

---

1. Revelation 21:23

2. Revelation 22:1-5

All covenants and promises that the Lord has made have been fulfilled:

- The seed of the woman (Christ) has crushed the head of the serpent as He promised to Adam and Eve.

- All nations have been blessed as He promised Abraham in the Abrahamic Covenant.

- Jesus is *the root and the descendant of David* and He is sitting on the throne forever as promised in the Davidic Covenant.

- New Jerusalem is in the land that God covenanted to Abraham and renewed in the Palestinian Covenant.

- All evil has been punished and the believers rewarded with a new heart and a new spirit as promised in the New Covenant.

And there will be no remembrance of the old age for, behold, I create new heavens and a new Earth; and the former shall not be remembered nor come into mind. [3]

God, in the beginning created the heavens and the earth. Now, we have a new heaven and new earth and here there is no evil, no sin, and no rebellion. Here there is only a holy God and the people He has made holy living together forever.

All has been restored. All that is left now is eternity with God.

And there will no longer be any night; and they will not have need of the light of a lamp nor the light of the sun, because the Lord God will illumine them; and they will reign forever and ever. [4]

He is the Alpha and the Omega – the beginning and the end.

As the book started with God reigning it closes the same way. In the beginning was God and forever and ever there will be God. And His people adore Him and live forever with Him in peace and the joy of His presence.

---

3. Isaiah 65:17

4. Revelation 22:5

Praise God. Worship our Lord. Serve your King. We will be with Him soon.

> *Yes, I am coming quickly. Amen. Come, Lord Jesus. The grace of the Lord Jesus be with all. Amen.*[5]

5. Revelation 22:20

EPILOGUE

One story, one God Almighty. You now have the big overview of all He has planned for our salvation and His glory.

We are blessed to live in a time where we can see the big picture. We can see the hand of God moving throughout time and throughout life today, where we are in His story and where He is taking us. We are almost to the end of the story and the end is known to us.

We have read ahead to see the completion of all of God's promises, the defeat of all of His enemies and the promise of life forever with Him. Do not fear what is to come for it will be just a closing moment in His great story. And then, we shall be with Him forever.

Our God is mighty to save. He has saved you. And you shall see His full salvation very soon. Walk worthy of your calling for the rest of your days. Walk closely with your God and one day we shall all be together with Him for eternity.

All praise to our God. All praise to our King. There is no other God but Him.

How should we then live?

What's Next?

Foundations of Faith

Our God is infinite and His Word is alive. The more we know of Him through His Word the greater our transformation and our joy.

If you want to go deeper, learn more and grow in your faith, I have a set of books called, "Foundations of Faith" that will give you a solid place to stand in knowledge and in daily life. This book, "The Bible Understood" is one of the four. Here are the other three:

"Is Your God Too Small? – your guide to a powerful knowledge of God and a deep relationship with Him."

- Know your God – who He says that He is.

"I'm a New Creation – how to transform your old ways and live as the amazing new you."

- Know who you are in Christ -what does it mean to be a new creation and how to live it every day.

"Spiritual Warfare – discover the lies used to separate you from God and the truth that sets you free."

- Know your enemy – discover his tactics so that you are equipped to beat him at his own game. Don't let him discourage you or separate you from God.

<u>The Foundations of Faith System</u> is a powerful method to build your faith, your connection to the in Lord and your love for Him.

Find more information at:

https://courses.drkimwest.info/courses/foundations-of-faith

Enter FAITH12OFF in the coupon box for $12 off the price of the system.

ALSO BY KIM WEST PHD MDIV

Dr. Kim's writings are designed to take you deeper in understanding God, His Word and how to make your Christian life work.

You will find her current books listed below and at https://shop.drkimwest.orgExpect to see new books and courses listed almost monthly.

Bible Study

Is Your God Too Small? – your guide to a powerful knowledge of God and a deep relationship with Him

Spiritual Warfare – discover the lies used to separate you from God and the truth that set you free

I'm a New Creation – how to transform your old ways and live as the amazing new you

The Deception of Adam – unveiling satan's strategy to divide God's people

Counseling/Life Coaching

Released From Fear – discover the simple and powerful path to an anxiety-free life

Guilt-Free Boundaries – how to set healthy Christian boundaries and have peace without apology

No More Panic Attacks – learn to calm your body, quiet your mind and reclaim your life

Silence Your Inner Bully – and create a peaceful mind

Healthy Self-Love – in a narcissistic world

Balance – the essential guide to a Christian life that works

Silence Your Inner Bully – and create a peaceful mind

Spiritual Disciplines and Devotionals

Silence and Solitude – come away with God

In His Presence – your guide to a joyful daily life with God

Simplicity – making space for God

Conversations with God – a deeper method of Bible study

The Simple Devotional Vol #1 – bite sized but transformational. Deep yet straightforward

Coming Soon

The Restoration of Eve – An In-Depth Look At Women Through the eyes of Christ (2024)

The Repentance of the Church – acknowledging and righting the wrongs committed against women (coming 2025)

The Simple Devotional Vol #2 - bite sized but transformational. Deep yet straightforward (coming 2025)

One Year to the Best You Ever – the "get specific" blueprint

Break Free of People Pleasing – quickly learn to stop living for the approval of others

Life Success Method – stop dreaming and start doing

Take Control of Your Mind – stop reacting, control triggers and create a powerful mind

https://shop.drkimwest.org

ABOUT THE AUTHOR

 Since the Lord came into her life that morning in Boulder, Colorado, Dr. Kim has not been the same. It was as if color came into a gray world for the first time and she wanted to fully understand what had happened and glorify God for it.

She set out to know this God, to understand His word and to let it shape her thinking and her world. For over four decades she has followed hard after God.

God called her to go to seminary to get a deeper understanding and equip her to teach others what she discovered. After receiving her Master of Divinity, He then called her to continue her study leading her to obtain a PhD in Clinical Pastoral Counseling.

Kim's focus has been on removing every obstacle to a joyful life in Christ. That has meant counseling to heal the soul, teaching to empower the mind and life coaching on how to live the abundant, powerful, joy-filled life in Christ that He came to give to us.

Writing has been a way to share her knowledge, expertise and experience in how to live mightily with God. She is focused on publishing the 27 books she has written and she will also publish the 12 books she is currently working on.

If you would like to join her email to know of new books and to receive a FREE ebook, "Is Your Life Too Small," just enter your email here: https://drkimwest.info/is-your-life-too-small